# Securing APIs: Protocols and Practice

James Relington

# DEDICATION

To those who seek knowledge, inspiration, and new perspectives—
may this book be a companion on your journey, a spark for curiosity,
and a reminder that every page turned is a step toward discovery.

# AKNOWLEDGEMENTS

I would like to express my deepest gratitude to everyone who contributed to the creation of this book. To my colleagues and mentors, your insights and expertise have been invaluable. A special thank you to my family and friends for their unwavering support and encouragement throughout this journey.

# Understanding API Security Fundamentals

In today's digital landscape, Application Programming Interfaces, or APIs, are essential components of modern software architectures. They serve as the bridges between systems, enabling applications to communicate, share data, and execute functions in a streamlined and standardized manner. From mobile apps to web services and cloud infrastructures, APIs are everywhere. However, their ubiquity also makes them attractive targets for malicious actors. Understanding the fundamentals of API security is crucial for developers, architects, and security professionals aiming to build robust and resilient systems that stand up against evolving threats.

API security is not merely about protecting the endpoints that serve data. It involves securing the entire lifecycle of an API, including its design, deployment, usage, and eventual retirement. APIs often expose critical functions and data that, if improperly secured, could lead to severe breaches. These risks make APIs one of the top attack vectors for cybercriminals, as evidenced by countless high-profile incidents involving stolen data, compromised credentials, and unauthorized access to internal systems. Therefore, securing APIs begins with a solid understanding of the core principles that guide API development and integration.

One of the foundational concepts in API security is identity verification. APIs need to know who or what is making a request, which makes authentication a primary concern. Authentication ensures that only users or systems with proper credentials can access an API. There are various methods for achieving this, ranging from simple API keys to complex multi-factor authentication schemes. The strength of the authentication mechanism must match the sensitivity of the API and the data it exposes. Weak or missing authentication is one of the most common vulnerabilities found in public-facing APIs.

Closely tied to authentication is the concept of authorization, which determines what an authenticated entity is allowed to do. An API must enforce strict access control policies to ensure users can only access the resources and perform the actions they are permitted to. Role-based access control (RBAC) and attribute-based access control (ABAC) are two widely used models in this domain. The failure to implement proper authorization controls can result in privilege escalation and data leaks, potentially exposing sensitive information to unauthorized users.

Another critical aspect of API security is the protection of data during transmission. APIs often transmit data over networks that may not be fully secure. To safeguard the confidentiality and integrity of this data, APIs should always use HTTPS, which encrypts communication using the TLS protocol. Without encryption, data such as passwords, tokens, or personally identifiable information can be intercepted by attackers in transit. Ensuring the correct implementation and configuration of TLS is therefore a non-negotiable step in securing API traffic.

Input validation is another fundamental element in the secure design of APIs. APIs must never trust client-provided input blindly. Attackers can exploit weak input validation to inject malicious payloads, manipulate queries, or crash services. Common threats such as SQL injection, XML injection, and cross-site scripting (XSS) can originate from improperly validated data. Strong input validation involves checking the type, format, length, and content of all incoming data before processing it. This defensive programming practice helps mitigate a wide array of potential attack vectors.

Monitoring and logging API activity is an essential operational aspect of security. Real-time monitoring can detect unusual or suspicious behavior, such as excessive request rates or repeated failed login attempts. Logging provides a historical record that can aid in forensic investigations after a security incident. However, it is important to ensure that logs do not contain sensitive information, such as plaintext credentials or personal user data. Secure logging practices help maintain visibility into API usage while also preserving the confidentiality of data.

Rate limiting and throttling are techniques used to control the flow of requests to an API. These mechanisms help prevent abuse by limiting the number of requests a client can make within a given timeframe. By implementing these controls, developers can mitigate risks such as denial-of-service (DoS) attacks and brute-force attempts. Rate limiting also ensures that system resources are distributed fairly among users and that one user or client does not monopolize access to the API.

Error handling and message responses play a subtle yet significant role in API security. APIs should avoid exposing too much information in error messages, as detailed error outputs can provide attackers with insights into system internals, database structures, or software configurations. Generic error responses that do not reveal implementation details are preferred. Additionally, APIs should be designed to fail securely, ensuring that unexpected or malformed requests do not cause the system to behave in unpredictable ways.

Security testing is a recurring practice that should be integrated into the development lifecycle of APIs. Static analysis tools, dynamic scanners, and penetration testing techniques can help identify vulnerabilities early and provide developers with actionable feedback. By incorporating security testing into CI/CD pipelines, organizations can ensure that new code changes do not introduce regressions or open new attack surfaces. This shift-left approach to security emphasizes prevention over detection, reducing the likelihood of vulnerabilities reaching production environments.

Education and awareness are also key components of API security fundamentals. Developers must be trained in secure coding practices, and organizations should foster a culture that prioritizes security at every level of development. Security policies, coding standards, and architectural guidelines should be clearly documented and communicated. Moreover, security is not a one-time activity but a continuous process. Threat landscapes evolve, and new vulnerabilities emerge regularly, necessitating constant vigilance and adaptation.

Ultimately, understanding API security fundamentals requires a holistic mindset that encompasses technical practices, operational controls, and cultural values. A secure API is one that has been thoughtfully designed, rigorously tested, and continuously monitored. By mastering these core principles, organizations can build APIs that not only deliver functionality but also protect the integrity, confidentiality, and availability of the systems they support.

# The Role of Authentication in API Protection

Authentication is one of the most critical pillars in the security of Application Programming Interfaces. It serves as the first line of defense against unauthorized access and malicious activity. When a client attempts to interact with an API, the system must be able to verify who or what is making the request before any resources are made accessible. This process is essential to ensure that only legitimate users or systems are allowed to access sensitive data or perform privileged operations. Without proper authentication mechanisms, APIs become open doors for attackers to exploit, manipulate, or exfiltrate information.

The concept of authentication in API protection is deeply tied to identity. The primary goal of authentication is to establish confidence that the entity interacting with the API is indeed who it claims to be. This identity can belong to a human user, a device, a service, or another system component. The process involves presenting some form of credential or token that can be verified by the API backend. Once the identity has been confirmed, the API can proceed to check what actions that identity is authorized to perform, which is the domain of authorization.

There are multiple authentication methods available, each with its own strengths, weaknesses, and appropriate use cases. One of the most basic forms is the use of API keys. These are unique identifiers issued to clients and are typically passed in the request header or as a URL parameter. While simple to implement, API keys offer limited security, especially if they are not rotated regularly or if they are embedded in publicly accessible client-side code. They do not provide any inherent mechanism for user identity or session tracking, which makes them unsuitable for complex authentication needs or systems requiring granular access control.

More advanced authentication protocols include OAuth 2.0 and OpenID Connect. OAuth 2.0 is a widely adopted standard that enables third-party applications to access a user's resources without exposing the user's credentials. It operates using access tokens, which are issued by an authorization server after the client is successfully authenticated. These tokens are then included in API requests to grant access to specific resources. OpenID Connect builds on top of OAuth 2.0 to provide authentication in addition to authorization, allowing clients to verify the identity of the user through the use of ID tokens. These modern protocols are particularly effective in scenarios involving user delegation, social logins, or mobile app integrations.

Another powerful method for securing APIs is mutual TLS, also known as two-way SSL. Unlike standard HTTPS, where only the client verifies the server's certificate, mutual TLS involves both the client and server validating each other's identities using digital certificates. This approach is highly secure and is often used in internal API communications between services within trusted networks. However, it can be complex to manage, especially at scale, due to the need for certificate issuance, renewal, and revocation.

JWT, or JSON Web Tokens, are another common tool in the authentication landscape. These compact, URL-safe tokens contain claims that represent user identity and permissions. Once issued, they can be passed between systems and verified using a digital signature. JWTs are stateless, which means the server does not need to store session information, making them efficient for scaling APIs. However, their use must be carefully managed, as long-lived tokens can pose a security risk if compromised, and improper validation can open the door to token forgery or replay attacks.

A secure authentication mechanism must also consider token lifecycle management. This includes ensuring that tokens expire after a reasonable period and providing mechanisms to revoke them when necessary, such as during logout or when suspicious activity is detected. Refresh tokens can be used to extend sessions securely without forcing users to reauthenticate frequently, but their use must be carefully restricted and protected to avoid abuse.

In modern API ecosystems, authentication is often handled through a centralized identity provider. This identity provider can offer Single Sign-On capabilities and integrate with external services for federation, such as LDAP directories or social login platforms. Centralized authentication offers the benefit of consistency and ease of auditing, as all identity-related actions are logged in a single location. It also simplifies the integration of additional security features such as multi-factor authentication, which adds an extra layer of protection by requiring a second factor, such as a text message code or biometric scan.

When designing authentication for APIs, developers must also take into account the potential for threats such as brute-force attacks, credential stuffing, and phishing. Implementing rate limiting, monitoring failed login attempts, and using CAPTCHA challenges can mitigate many of these risks. It is also important to ensure that authentication endpoints themselves are secure and resistant to enumeration, where attackers can discover valid usernames by observing subtle differences in error messages.

One of the often overlooked aspects of API authentication is the secure storage and handling of secrets. Hardcoding credentials in code repositories or configuration files can expose APIs to unnecessary risk. Secrets should be stored in secure vaults or environment variables, encrypted at rest, and never transmitted in plaintext. Automated scanning tools can help detect exposed secrets in codebases before they reach production environments.

Authentication should also be implemented consistently across all APIs within an organization. Discrepancies in authentication mechanisms between services can create gaps in the security architecture, allowing attackers to exploit the weakest link. It is essential to maintain a clear and enforceable authentication policy that is reviewed regularly and updated as new threats and standards emerge.

Ultimately, the role of authentication in API protection is to serve as a gatekeeper, ensuring that every request is made by a known and verified entity. It is the cornerstone upon which further security measures, such as authorization, encryption, and auditing, are built. A well-designed authentication system reduces the attack surface of APIs, enhances user trust, and lays the foundation for a resilient and secure API infrastructure. By investing in strong authentication practices, organizations can dramatically improve their ability to safeguard digital assets and maintain the integrity of their services.

# Authorization Models for Secure API Access

Authorization is the process of determining what actions an authenticated user or system is allowed to perform. While authentication confirms identity, authorization defines permissions. In the context of API security, authorization models are the frameworks and strategies used to enforce access control, ensuring that only approved entities can interact with certain endpoints, read specific data, or execute protected operations. The strength and appropriateness of an authorization model directly affect the overall security posture of an API. A well-designed authorization layer prevents unauthorized data exposure, misuse of functionality, and privilege escalation. Insecure or misconfigured authorization, on the other hand, can open the door to devastating data breaches and system compromise.

At the heart of every authorization model is the concept of policy enforcement. Policies dictate who can do what under which conditions. These policies must be clearly defined, consistently applied, and thoroughly tested to be effective. In APIs, these policies are typically enforced at the endpoint level, meaning the server checks the permissions associated with the requester before granting access to any resource. The implementation of authorization must be as granular as the business logic requires, allowing for control over specific methods, data fields, or actions. Granularity is critical, especially in systems that handle sensitive or personal data, where overly permissive access can have serious privacy and compliance consequences.

One of the most widely used models in API authorization is Role-Based Access Control, or RBAC. In RBAC, access decisions are based on roles assigned to users. Each role defines a set of permissions, and users inherit access rights through their role membership. For example, an employee might have the role of admin, editor, or viewer, each of which comes with different levels of access to the API's functionality. RBAC is relatively straightforward to implement and works well in systems with clearly defined user hierarchies. However, it can become inflexible in dynamic environments where access needs to adapt to context or change frequently.

Attribute-Based Access Control, or ABAC, expands on the capabilities of RBAC by considering various attributes associated with the user, the resource, the action, and the environment. These attributes could include a user's department, location, time of access, or even device type. ABAC allows for more fine-grained and context-aware policies. For example, a policy might allow access only during business hours or only from a company-issued device. This model is powerful in complex enterprise environments, but it also introduces additional complexity in terms of policy definition, evaluation, and management.

Another model gaining traction in API security is Policy-Based Access Control, sometimes referred to as PBAC or ReBAC when relationships are taken into account. This approach separates policy logic from application code and uses a centralized policy engine to evaluate requests against defined rules. This decoupling makes policies easier to update and audit. It also facilitates compliance with regulatory requirements, as organizations can demonstrate exactly how access decisions are made. Policy engines like Open Policy Agent are increasingly used in cloud-native environments to implement PBAC in a flexible and scalable way.

Scoping is an important concept in token-based authorization models, particularly in OAuth 2.0. Scopes define what an access token is permitted to do. When a client requests a token, it specifies the desired scope, such as read access to user data or permission to modify a resource. The authorization server evaluates the request and returns a token with the appropriate scope, which the API uses to enforce access control. This mechanism allows for least privilege by ensuring that tokens grant only the minimum permissions necessary for a given operation. Proper scoping helps mitigate the impact of a compromised token by limiting what an attacker could do with it.

In systems where APIs expose multi-tenant functionality, access isolation becomes especially important. Authorization must ensure that users can only access resources that belong to their own organization or account. This is often referred to as tenancy isolation. Any failure in tenancy-based access control could lead to data leaks between customers, which can be catastrophic for trust and regulatory compliance. Multi-tenant authorization requires careful design, including consistent checks for tenant ownership on every data access and operation. Implementing this properly may involve tagging data with tenant identifiers and enforcing strict validation of user claims.

Fine-grained authorization is often implemented through permission checks embedded directly in the application logic. For example, even after verifying that a user is authenticated and has the correct role, the system might need to check whether they own the specific resource being accessed. This kind of ownership verification is essential to prevent horizontal privilege escalation, where users gain access to data or functions belonging to other users. Fine-grained checks must be systematic and consistent across the API to ensure no endpoint is left unguarded.

Auditing and logging of authorization decisions play a crucial role in maintaining security and accountability. Every access attempt, whether successful or denied, should be logged with sufficient detail to support investigations and detect anomalies. These logs provide invaluable insight into how access policies are being used in practice and can highlight misconfigurations or unexpected usage patterns. They also support compliance efforts by offering a clear record of data access and administrative actions.

Authorization must also be integrated into the software development lifecycle. Security cannot be an afterthought or a separate component bolted onto an application after development is complete. Developers should be trained to implement secure access control from the beginning, and policies should be defined in collaboration with security teams and stakeholders who understand the sensitivity of the data involved. Continuous testing, including automated security testing and manual reviews, is necessary to ensure that access control remains effective as the application evolves.

As threats evolve and systems become more interconnected, the need for robust and adaptive authorization models continues to grow. APIs must be built with security embedded at every level, and authorization is a key enabler of that vision. It empowers organizations to enforce business rules, comply with data protection regulations, and maintain trust with users. The right authorization model depends on the specific needs of the application, the complexity of access requirements, and the level of sensitivity of the resources involved. By carefully choosing, implementing, and maintaining an appropriate authorization strategy, API developers and security teams can protect their systems against misuse, abuse, and unauthorized access.

# API Keys: Simplicity and Security Trade-offs

API keys are one of the oldest and simplest mechanisms for securing access to Application Programming Interfaces. Their straightforward design and ease of implementation have made them a popular choice among developers, particularly when building quick prototypes, internal tools, or third-party integrations. At their core, API keys are unique identifiers issued by an API provider to clients, allowing the provider to distinguish between different consumers and control access to its services. These keys are usually included in the request headers, query parameters, or body of API calls and are checked on the server side to determine whether access should be granted. While this model provides a basic level of protection, it also introduces significant limitations and risks when used in more demanding or sensitive environments.

The simplicity of API keys is both their greatest strength and their most glaring weakness. On the one hand, generating and issuing an API key requires minimal effort. The server assigns a unique string to a client, and as long as the client includes that string in subsequent requests, the server can associate the traffic with a specific user, application, or organization. This level of simplicity means that developers can get up and running quickly without needing to implement more complex authentication flows or identity management infrastructure. For many low-risk use cases, such as accessing public or semi-public data, this lightweight approach may be entirely sufficient.

However, simplicity comes at the cost of flexibility and security. API keys lack the ability to distinguish between users within the same client, which means they cannot be used for fine-grained authorization or user-specific data access without significant additional effort. They also do not inherently support features like expiration, rotation, or revocation, unless these capabilities are implemented manually. This can make them brittle and difficult to manage at scale, especially when dealing with a large number of clients or when responding to a potential key compromise.

One of the primary concerns with API keys is that they function essentially like passwords. If someone obtains a valid API key, they can make requests to the API as if they were the legitimate client. Unlike more advanced authentication mechanisms that rely on short-lived tokens, public-private key pairs, or mutual TLS, API keys are often long-lived and static. This makes them particularly attractive targets for attackers. If a key is accidentally exposed in a public code repository, logged in error messages, or transmitted over an unencrypted connection, it can be immediately exploited unless countermeasures are in place.

The lack of context-awareness in API keys also introduces challenges. API keys do not natively carry information about the requester, such as their location, device, or intended action. As a result, APIs using only keys for access control are often limited to making binary decisions—either the key is valid or it is not. This limits the ability to implement adaptive security measures or contextual risk analysis, both of which are becoming increasingly important in modern systems. Additional layers, such as IP allowlists or rate limiting, must often be introduced to compensate for the key's lack of intelligence.

Another issue is that many developers, especially those new to API design, treat API keys as sufficient on their own, unaware of their limitations. This can lead to APIs being deployed in production with inadequate security controls, increasing the risk of unauthorized access and abuse. In environments where sensitive data is exposed, such as personal user information, financial records, or health data, relying solely on API keys is generally considered insufficient. These scenarios demand stronger authentication and authorization mechanisms that can verify both the identity and the permissions of each requester.

Despite these shortcomings, API keys can still play a valuable role when used appropriately and with supporting controls. One best practice is to scope API keys to limit their access. Instead of giving a key full access to all resources and endpoints, it can be restricted to specific operations or paths. This minimizes the potential damage in the event of a key being compromised. Another important control is enforcing expiration and rotation policies. Keys should be time-bound and periodically regenerated, reducing the window of opportunity for misuse. Automating this process can help ensure that developers do not forget to replace old or compromised keys.

Monitoring and analytics also become essential when managing API keys at scale. Providers should track usage patterns associated with each key to detect anomalies that may indicate abuse or unauthorized access. Sudden spikes in traffic, access from unusual geographic locations, or attempts to hit unauthorized endpoints can all serve as red flags. Alerting systems can be configured to notify administrators when suspicious activity is detected, allowing them to respond quickly by revoking or rotating affected keys.

Many organizations choose to pair API keys with additional security layers rather than rely on them alone. For example, an API might require a valid key as a baseline check but then enforce OAuth 2.0 for user-specific operations. In such hybrid models, the key functions more like a gatekeeper, ensuring that only registered clients can interact with the API at all, while more sensitive transactions require robust, user-level authentication and authorization. This layered approach balances ease of use with stronger security protections where they matter most.

API keys are also sometimes used in conjunction with digital signing. In this setup, the API key is used to generate a hash of the request payload, which the server can then verify using the same key. This prevents tampering and ensures the integrity of the message, although it does not address the core issues of identity and permissions. For APIs that handle financial transactions or time-sensitive data, implementing signed requests can add an important layer of trust and accountability.

Ultimately, the choice to use API keys must be informed by a clear understanding of the trade-offs involved. While they offer a quick and accessible entry point to API security, their limitations must not be ignored. Developers and architects must assess the sensitivity of the data being exposed, the number and diversity of clients, and the operational overhead of managing keys over time. When combined with other controls such as scope restrictions, rate limits, IP filtering, and layered authentication, API keys can still serve as a useful tool. However, they should never be mistaken for a comprehensive security solution in and of themselves. Understanding both their capabilities and their limitations is essential for any organization seeking to build APIs that are both user-friendly and secure.

# OAuth 2.0: Delegated Authorization Explained

OAuth 2.0 is a widely adopted authorization framework that enables third-party applications to gain limited access to user resources without needing to collect or store the user's credentials. This model, known as delegated authorization, addresses one of the core challenges in modern API security: how to allow a service to perform actions or access data on behalf of a user while preserving security, control, and privacy. Instead of sharing passwords or full account access, users grant applications specific permissions through tokens issued by an authorization server. This division of roles and responsibilities is what makes OAuth 2.0 a cornerstone in the secure design of APIs, especially in distributed and cloud-based environments.

The OAuth 2.0 framework defines four key roles: the resource owner, the client, the resource server, and the authorization server. The resource owner is typically the user who owns the data or service being accessed. The client is the application that wants to access the resource on behalf of the user. The resource server hosts the protected resources, and the authorization server is responsible for authenticating the resource owner and issuing access tokens to the client. This structure allows a clean separation of concerns, making it easier to implement and manage access control across diverse systems.

One of the most common real-world examples of OAuth 2.0 is when a user allows a third-party application to access their email, calendar, or social media data. Instead of handing over their password, the user is redirected to a secure login page hosted by the identity provider. After authenticating and approving the requested permissions, the user is redirected back to the third-party application along with an authorization code. This code is then exchanged by the client for an access token, which can be used to make authorized API requests on the user's behalf. At no point does the client handle or store the user's actual credentials, which significantly reduces the attack surface and potential for abuse.

OAuth 2.0 supports several different authorization flows to accommodate different types of clients and use cases. The Authorization Code Flow is used primarily by server-side web applications, while the Implicit Flow was historically used by browser-based applications but is now considered less secure and largely deprecated. The Resource Owner Password Credentials Flow, which involves the user giving their credentials directly to the client, is also discouraged in modern architectures due to its inherent risks. The Client Credentials Flow, on the other hand, is suitable for service-to-service communication where no user is involved, and access is granted based on the client's own identity.

The access token is at the heart of OAuth 2.0's authorization mechanism. Once issued, this token represents the permissions granted by the user to the client. It is included in API requests as a bearer token, typically in the Authorization header, and allows the resource server to verify the legitimacy of the request. These tokens are often JSON Web Tokens (JWTs), which are compact, signed data structures that can carry metadata and claims about the user and the scope of access. While self-contained JWTs are useful for stateless validation, they also require careful handling, especially regarding expiration, revocation, and validation of digital signatures.

Scope management is another essential feature of OAuth 2.0. Scopes define the boundaries of what the access token can do. For example, an application might request read-only access to a user's contacts or permission to send emails on their behalf. By presenting a clear and limited set of scopes, OAuth 2.0 enables users to make informed decisions about what data they are sharing and with whom. The principle of least privilege is inherently supported through scopes, ensuring that clients only receive the access they truly need.

OAuth 2.0 also supports refresh tokens, which are used to obtain new access tokens without requiring the user to reauthenticate. This is especially useful for maintaining long-lived sessions in mobile or desktop applications. Refresh tokens are more sensitive than access tokens because they can be used to mint new tokens, potentially indefinitely. Therefore, they must be stored securely, transmitted only over encrypted channels, and revoked immediately if any suspicion of compromise arises. Best practices dictate issuing short-lived access tokens and longer-lived refresh tokens, thus balancing usability with security.

Security concerns in OAuth 2.0 implementations often stem not from the protocol itself but from incorrect configurations or incomplete implementations. Redirect URI manipulation, token leakage, and lack of proper validation are common mistakes that can be exploited by attackers. It is critical to ensure that redirect URIs are exact matches, that tokens are stored and transmitted securely, and that all parties validate signatures and token claims appropriately. Developers should also ensure that Cross-Site Request Forgery (CSRF) protection is implemented, particularly in flows that involve user-agent redirection.

OAuth 2.0 is frequently used in conjunction with OpenID Connect, which extends the framework to include authentication capabilities. While OAuth 2.0 by itself is strictly about authorization, OpenID Connect introduces the ID token, which provides verified information about the user. This combination allows applications not only to act on behalf of a user but also to identify the user securely. As such, OpenID Connect is now the de facto standard for implementing both authentication and authorization in web and mobile applications.

Deploying OAuth 2.0 in a secure and user-friendly way requires careful planning and adherence to best practices. Token storage must be handled securely, especially in client-side environments. Communication with authorization and resource servers must be encrypted using TLS. Audit logs should capture token issuance, usage, and revocation events to support traceability and incident response. Access should be regularly reviewed, and users should be able to revoke permissions easily. Centralized consent management portals are a valuable addition, giving users control and transparency over the third-party applications they have authorized.

The flexibility of OAuth 2.0 has led to its adoption across industries and platforms. From single sign-on implementations in enterprises to secure third-party integrations in consumer applications, OAuth 2.0 continues to be a vital component of modern API ecosystems. Its delegated authorization model supports scalability, improves user privacy, and allows developers to build secure applications without being responsible for handling sensitive credentials. Despite its complexity and the potential for misconfiguration, when implemented properly, OAuth 2.0 offers a robust and secure method for managing access in distributed, interconnected environments.

# OpenID Connect for Identity Verification

OpenID Connect is a modern authentication protocol built on top of the OAuth 2.0 framework, designed to solve one of the most fundamental challenges in digital systems: verifying the identity of users in a secure, interoperable, and scalable manner. While OAuth 2.0 is focused strictly on delegated authorization—granting applications access to resources without revealing user credentials—OpenID Connect extends this capability by enabling authentication and delivering verified identity information to client applications. It allows developers to authenticate users across systems and domains using a single protocol, reducing friction, improving security, and simplifying the implementation of federated identity solutions. OpenID Connect is now one of the most widely used standards for identity verification, powering everything from enterprise single sign-on systems to consumer login experiences on popular websites and mobile apps.

At its core, OpenID Connect introduces an additional token to the OAuth 2.0 flow: the ID token. Unlike the access token, which is used to authorize access to protected resources, the ID token contains identity-related claims about the user, such as their unique identifier, name, email, and other profile information. This token is digitally signed by the identity provider, enabling the client application to validate that the information has not been tampered with and that it comes from a trusted source. Because of this, client applications no longer need to manage their own authentication logic or credential storage, greatly reducing the attack surface and development complexity.

The process begins when a user attempts to log in to a client application. Instead of prompting the user to enter credentials directly, the application redirects the user to an identity provider, also known as the OpenID Provider. The identity provider handles authentication, which may include multi-factor authentication, biometric checks, or integration with external identity sources such as LDAP or social login providers. Once the user has been authenticated successfully, the provider redirects the user back to the application along with an authorization code. The application then exchanges this code with the identity provider's token endpoint to receive an ID token, and optionally an access token and refresh token, depending on the requested scopes and flow.

The ID token is central to the identity verification process in OpenID Connect. It is typically formatted as a JSON Web Token, or JWT, which is a compact, URL-safe structure consisting of a header, payload, and signature. The payload contains standard claims, such as the subject identifier (sub), issuer (iss), audience (aud), expiration time (exp), and authentication timestamp (auth_time). It may also contain additional claims if requested, such as the user's name or preferred username. By validating the signature and checking that the claims match the expected values, the client can confirm that the token is legitimate and that the user's identity has been verified.

One of the key advantages of OpenID Connect is that it enables federated identity. Instead of maintaining separate usernames and passwords for each application, users can authenticate using a central identity provider. This approach streamlines user management, improves usability, and strengthens security by allowing organizations to enforce consistent authentication policies across all connected applications. Single sign-on becomes possible, where users can authenticate once and gain access to multiple systems without needing to log in again. This not only enhances user experience but also reduces the likelihood of password reuse and phishing attacks.

OpenID Connect supports several authentication flows, allowing it to be used in a variety of application environments. The Authorization Code Flow is the most secure and is recommended for server-side applications. It ensures that tokens are exchanged directly between servers, minimizing the risk of token interception. The Implicit Flow was once used in client-side applications such as single-page applications, but it is now discouraged due to its exposure of tokens in browser environments. The newer Authorization Code Flow with Proof Key for Code Exchange (PKCE) has become the preferred choice for mobile and browser-based apps, offering enhanced security by requiring a dynamically generated secret during the token exchange process.

Security considerations in OpenID Connect implementations are paramount. Applications must ensure that they verify the ID token's signature, check the issuer and audience fields, and validate expiration and nonce claims. The nonce is a randomly generated value included in the authentication request and echoed in the ID token, protecting against replay attacks. Developers must also take care not to expose tokens in browser history, logs, or unsecured storage. Using HTTPS for all communication, applying proper session management practices, and implementing logout flows to terminate sessions securely are all essential components of a secure OpenID Connect deployment.

User consent is another important feature of OpenID Connect. When an application requests access to identity data, the identity provider presents a consent screen where the user can review and approve the requested scopes. These scopes may include openid, which is required for all OpenID Connect requests, along with profile, email, address, and phone. This consent mechanism supports user privacy by making data sharing explicit and giving users control over what information is shared and with which applications. Consent records can be managed by the identity provider and revoked at any time, providing users with ongoing transparency and autonomy.

OpenID Connect is not limited to human users. It can also be used for machine-to-machine authentication in some scenarios, particularly when client identities need to be verified as part of a broader zero-trust architecture. Service accounts, for example, can authenticate and receive ID tokens with associated claims that help downstream services make informed authorization decisions. This machine identity verification is essential in modern cloud-native applications where services dynamically interact across networks and boundaries.

Interoperability is a core design principle of OpenID Connect. The protocol is designed to work across platforms, devices, and languages, with numerous libraries and toolkits available for rapid integration. This has contributed to its widespread adoption among identity providers, including major technology companies, financial institutions, and government services. OpenID Connect has become the backbone of identity federation on the internet, enabling users to log in securely to multiple services using a single trusted provider.

The protocol also continues to evolve. New specifications such as OpenID Connect Front-Channel Logout, Back-Channel Logout, and Session Management aim to improve the handling of logout across systems. Identity assurance and verified claims are being introduced to support higher assurance levels for applications that require verified identity attributes. These ongoing developments reflect the growing importance of identity in both consumer and enterprise contexts, as organizations seek to balance usability, security, and compliance.

OpenID Connect transforms the way identity is managed and verified in API ecosystems. It simplifies authentication for developers, enhances security for users, and enables seamless integration across diverse applications and services. By adopting OpenID Connect, organizations can move away from fragmented identity systems and towards a unified, standards-based approach that supports modern digital experiences and resilient security practices.

# Mutual TLS for API Authentication

Mutual TLS, often abbreviated as mTLS, is a powerful and highly secure method for authenticating both clients and servers in API communication. While traditional Transport Layer Security (TLS) ensures that the server presents a valid certificate to prove its identity to the client, mutual TLS extends this mechanism by requiring the client to also present a certificate during the handshake process. This bilateral authentication process creates a trusted, cryptographically verified connection between both parties. In the context of API security, mTLS is especially valuable for securing communications between services, enforcing strong identity verification, and reducing the attack surface in distributed architectures.

The principle behind mutual TLS is rooted in the concept of trust based on certificates issued by a recognized Certificate Authority. Each party in the communication must possess a valid X.509 certificate and the corresponding private key. When a client initiates a connection with a server, the server presents its certificate. The client validates it using the trusted root certificate chain. In return, the client presents its certificate, and the server validates it in the same manner. Only if both parties successfully verify each other's certificates does the connection proceed. This mechanism ensures that both ends of the communication channel are authenticated before any sensitive data is exchanged.

One of the strongest advantages of mTLS is its ability to provide identity assurance at the transport layer, without relying on higher-level credentials such as passwords, tokens, or API keys. This is particularly useful in environments where APIs are consumed by other services rather than individual users. In microservices architectures, containerized applications, and service meshes, services frequently communicate with one another over internal APIs. In these cases, mTLS enables robust service-to-service authentication, making it extremely difficult for unauthorized or rogue services to impersonate legitimate ones.

Unlike bearer tokens or API keys, which can be intercepted or replayed if not handled carefully, mTLS authentication is tied to possession of a private key. This private key never leaves the secure environment of the client or server and cannot be forged or duplicated without significant effort. As a result, mutual TLS provides a higher level of assurance than many other authentication methods, making it ideal for use in regulated industries, critical infrastructure, and any system that demands strong non-repudiation and mutual trust.

However, deploying mutual TLS in an API ecosystem comes with operational complexities. Managing the lifecycle of certificates is one of the most significant challenges. Certificates need to be issued, distributed, rotated, and eventually revoked. In large systems with hundreds or thousands of microservices, this process can quickly become difficult to manage without automation. Tools such as automated certificate management systems, certificate authorities integrated into service meshes, and dynamic secrets engines can help address this issue by streamlining certificate provisioning and renewal processes.

Another consideration in mTLS deployments is the configuration of trust stores. Both clients and servers must maintain a list of trusted root or intermediate certificate authorities to validate incoming certificates. Improper configuration can lead to failed handshakes or acceptance of unauthorized entities. Care must be taken to ensure that the trust stores are updated regularly and only contain trusted entities. Overly permissive trust stores increase the risk of accepting connections from unverified or compromised sources.

In environments where external clients access APIs, mutual TLS can be used to enforce client identity verification in a way that is transparent to the end user. For example, a business partner's system could be required to present a valid client certificate signed by a mutually trusted authority before accessing any endpoints. This is particularly useful for business-to-business APIs where human authentication is not practical and where automated systems must communicate securely on a regular basis. With proper certificate issuance and lifecycle management, mTLS creates a strong perimeter of trust that is difficult to bypass.

When integrated into service meshes such as Istio or Linkerd, mTLS becomes even more powerful. These service meshes provide automatic mTLS capabilities for all communication between services within the mesh. This means developers do not have to implement mTLS logic in their application code, and operations teams can manage encryption and authentication centrally. This model allows for consistent policy enforcement, simplified observability, and easier auditing of service communications, all while maintaining the benefits of strong mutual authentication.

It is important to understand the distinction between authentication and authorization in the context of mTLS. While mTLS provides strong authentication by verifying the identity of both the client and the server, it does not inherently define what that identity is allowed to do. Authorization must still be handled separately, typically by mapping the certificate subject or other attributes to access policies. For example, a certificate issued to a particular client might be associated with a limited set of API actions. Combining mTLS with policy engines or access control frameworks allows for fine-grained authorization decisions based on authenticated identities.

Logging and auditing are essential components of a secure mTLS-enabled API infrastructure. Every connection attempt, successful or failed, should be logged with relevant metadata such as certificate details, timestamp, and endpoint accessed. These logs can be used for detecting unauthorized access attempts, investigating incidents, and ensuring compliance with security policies. Because mTLS provides a cryptographically strong identity for each client, logs from mTLS-enabled systems are inherently more reliable and traceable than those based on less secure authentication methods.

From a performance perspective, mutual TLS introduces some overhead due to the additional steps involved in the handshake process. However, the impact is usually minimal in well-optimized systems and is often outweighed by the significant security benefits.

Proper tuning of TLS parameters and reuse of TLS sessions can help mitigate any performance penalties. Modern hardware and cryptographic libraries are optimized for TLS operations, making it feasible to use mTLS even in high-throughput environments.

Organizations adopting mTLS for API authentication must invest in proper education and tooling. Developers should understand how certificates work, what information they contain, and how to interpret errors related to TLS handshakes. Operations teams must have tools for monitoring certificate expiration, automating renewals, and validating configuration across distributed systems. With the right processes in place, mutual TLS becomes a scalable and resilient foundation for secure API communications.

Mutual TLS offers one of the most secure methods of API authentication available today. Its ability to provide strong, bidirectional identity verification makes it a valuable choice for systems that require high levels of trust, integrity, and confidentiality. While it comes with operational challenges, the security benefits of mTLS are substantial, especially when implemented with automation and integrated into broader security architectures. As APIs become the primary means of communication between services, adopting robust authentication methods like mutual TLS will be essential for building secure and trustworthy systems.

# Securing APIs with JWT Tokens

JSON Web Tokens, commonly known as JWTs, have become a foundational component of modern API security. These compact, URL-safe tokens allow for secure transmission of information between parties as a JSON object. They are digitally signed using a secret or a public/private key pair, enabling the recipient to verify the token's authenticity and integrity. JWTs are widely adopted in scenarios where stateless, scalable, and efficient authentication is required. Their use spans across single sign-on systems, authorization frameworks like OAuth 2.0 and OpenID Connect, and in securing microservices communication. As APIs become the primary method of exposing application functionality and data, securing them with JWTs offers a versatile and robust approach.

At a high level, a JWT consists of three parts: a header, a payload, and a signature. The header typically indicates the type of token and the algorithm used for signing. The payload contains the claims, which are statements about an entity (usually the user) and additional metadata. These claims may include standard fields such as the subject, issuer, expiration time, and issued-at timestamp, as well as custom claims relevant to the application's context. The signature is created by encoding the header and payload and signing them with a secret key or private key. When a server receives a JWT, it can verify the token's signature using the corresponding key and validate the claims to determine whether the request should be allowed.

One of the most compelling benefits of JWTs is their stateless nature. Because all necessary information is embedded within the token itself, servers do not need to maintain a session store or database lookup for every request. This characteristic makes JWTs ideal for distributed architectures and cloud-native applications where scalability and performance are paramount. Servers can decode and validate tokens independently without requiring shared state or central session storage, simplifying the infrastructure and reducing latency. However, this statelessness also introduces challenges, particularly in terms of revocation and token lifecycle management, which must be carefully addressed.

Token validation is a critical aspect of securing APIs with JWTs. The first step in validation is checking the token's signature to ensure that it has not been tampered with. If the token is signed with a symmetric key, both the issuer and the consumer must share the same secret. In asymmetric scenarios, the token is signed with a private key and verified using a public key, which is particularly useful when tokens are issued by a trusted identity provider and consumed by multiple independent services. After verifying the signature, the server must validate the claims. This includes checking the expiration time to ensure the token is still valid, verifying the issuer to confirm that the token came from a trusted source, and confirming the audience to make sure the token is intended for the recipient API.

The use of expiration times in JWTs introduces an important security control. Tokens should have a short lifespan to reduce the risk of abuse if they are intercepted or leaked. Short-lived tokens limit the window in which an attacker can use a stolen token, thereby enhancing overall security. In conjunction with access tokens, systems often use refresh tokens to maintain user sessions. Refresh tokens have a longer validity period and can be exchanged for new access tokens. Because refresh tokens grant the ability to obtain new access, they must be stored securely and used only over encrypted connections.

Scope management and permissions are commonly embedded in JWTs as part of the payload claims. This enables APIs to enforce fine-grained access control based on the token's contents. For example, a token may include a scope claim indicating whether the client can read, write, or delete specific resources. By inspecting these claims, the API can decide whether to permit or deny the request without needing to query a database or identity provider. This delegation of responsibility streamlines authorization and improves performance, though it also places greater importance on issuing tokens with accurate and minimal permissions.

While JWTs offer many benefits, they also come with security risks if not implemented correctly. One common mistake is failing to validate the token signature or blindly trusting tokens from unknown sources. Another is using weak or deprecated algorithms, such as the none algorithm, which can allow attackers to forge tokens if not properly blocked. It is essential to restrict supported algorithms to strong, vetted options and to explicitly validate each part of the token. Additionally, developers must avoid storing sensitive data in the payload, as JWTs are not encrypted by default. They are base64-encoded, which means the contents are easily viewable by anyone with access to the token. For confidentiality, data should be encrypted separately or the token should be transported securely using HTTPS.

Token reuse and replay attacks can also be a concern. Because JWTs are bearer tokens, possession equals access. If an attacker obtains a valid token, they can use it to impersonate the user. To mitigate this, systems should enforce HTTPS to prevent interception, use short-lived tokens to limit damage, and implement rate limiting or anomaly detection to identify suspicious behavior. Advanced solutions might include binding the token to a particular device or session or incorporating proof-of-possession mechanisms.

Another area requiring attention is token revocation. Because JWTs are stateless, there is no built-in way to revoke them once issued. This can be problematic if a user logs out, their account is compromised, or their access is otherwise revoked. One approach is to maintain a blacklist of revoked tokens or token identifiers, though this reintroduces state and must be managed carefully. Alternatively, systems can keep access tokens short-lived and use refresh tokens with revocation capabilities on the server side. Balancing stateless operation with revocation control is a nuanced aspect of designing secure JWT-based authentication.

The adoption of JWTs in API security continues to grow due to their performance benefits, flexibility, and ease of integration. They enable rapid and scalable authentication mechanisms that fit well within modern DevOps pipelines and cloud-native deployments. When used correctly, JWTs reduce overhead, improve user experience, and facilitate secure interactions between services and clients. Organizations that deploy JWTs must understand the token structure, carefully implement validation logic, and apply best practices in lifecycle management and claim handling to ensure that they gain the full security benefits without introducing unnecessary risks. Properly securing APIs with JWT tokens is not just about generating and signing tokens; it requires a thoughtful and disciplined approach to trust, cryptography, and system design.

# Managing Token Expiry and Revocation

In any secure API ecosystem, token management plays a vital role in maintaining control over access and ensuring that authenticated sessions do not persist longer than necessary. Tokens, whether in the form of JSON Web Tokens (JWTs), OAuth 2.0 access tokens, or session identifiers, act as digital passports that grant users and services the ability to interact with protected resources. However, like all security credentials, tokens must be governed by clear rules regarding their lifespan and the ability to invalidate them when necessary. Properly managing token expiry and revocation is essential to reducing security risks such as unauthorized access, token replay attacks, and privilege abuse.

Token expiry is a time-bound control mechanism that limits how long a token remains valid after it is issued. It is one of the most fundamental security features associated with token-based authentication systems. When a token has an expiration time defined, it enforces a boundary beyond which the token is no longer accepted by the server, even if it was originally valid. This reduces the potential impact of compromised tokens, as an attacker who obtains a stolen token would have only a limited window of opportunity to exploit it. Expiry times should be chosen based on the sensitivity of the operation and the trust level of the client. Short-lived tokens offer better security because they are less useful to an attacker over time. However, they also require more frequent re-authentication or token refreshes, which can affect usability and system complexity.

In many modern authentication flows, particularly those based on OAuth 2.0, token expiry is balanced by the introduction of refresh tokens. A refresh token is a long-lived credential that can be used to obtain new short-lived access tokens without requiring the user to re-authenticate. This design strikes a balance between user convenience and security. While access tokens may expire in minutes, refresh tokens may last hours, days, or even longer, depending on the use case. However, because refresh tokens grant the power to mint new access tokens, they must be treated with the utmost care. They should be stored securely, protected against theft, and revoked immediately if any suspicion of compromise arises.

Revocation is the act of explicitly invalidating a token before its expiry time has been reached. This can be necessary for many reasons. A user may log out of a system, terminating their session and requiring that no further requests be accepted with the old token. An administrator may need to revoke a token after detecting suspicious activity or policy violations. A user may reset their password, prompting a revocation of all existing tokens to prevent access with outdated credentials. In these and other scenarios, revocation provides a critical control point that allows the system to respond in real time to changing security conditions.

Managing revocation becomes particularly challenging in stateless token architectures. Tokens such as JWTs are self-contained and do not require server-side state. They are validated by verifying a digital signature and inspecting the token's claims. This makes them extremely efficient and scalable, as no lookup is needed to check whether the token is valid. However, it also means that once a token is issued, it remains valid until it expires, unless the server implements an external mechanism to track revoked tokens. Common approaches to solving this problem include maintaining a blacklist or revocation list of token identifiers or using short expiry times combined with refresh tokens that can be revoked more easily.

A revocation list introduces state into what is otherwise a stateless architecture. When a token is revoked, its identifier is added to a database or cache that the API checks before processing each request. This adds complexity and latency but ensures that tokens can be invalidated on demand. For high-throughput APIs, this list must be implemented using fast-access technologies such as in-memory key-value stores. In systems where millions of tokens are issued daily, pruning old entries and scaling the storage infrastructure becomes a critical consideration. A sliding time window or time-to-live mechanism can help manage the growth of the revocation list by automatically removing entries that correspond to tokens that would have expired naturally.

Another approach to token revocation is to use rotating refresh tokens. Instead of issuing a fixed refresh token that is used repeatedly, the system issues a new refresh token each time a new access token is generated. The old refresh token is invalidated immediately after use. This ensures that if an attacker steals a refresh token, they cannot use it if the legitimate user has already used it to obtain a new one. This model increases security but requires careful coordination between client and server, as clients must always store the latest refresh token and be prepared for scenarios where token rotation fails or is interrupted.

Token introspection is another technique used to manage revocation in systems where tokens are not self-contained. With introspection, the API does not validate the token locally. Instead, it sends the token to an authorization server, which checks its validity, status, and associated metadata before responding. This approach allows real-time revocation because the server can immediately respond that a token is no longer valid. The trade-off is increased latency and dependency on the availability of the introspection endpoint. It also introduces a central point of failure and may not scale well without optimization.

Auditing and monitoring are essential components of token management. Logging token issuance, usage, and revocation events provides visibility into the authentication lifecycle. These logs can be used to detect anomalies, such as a token being used from an unexpected geographic location or at unusual times. Security information and event management systems can ingest these logs to trigger alerts or automated responses when suspicious patterns are detected. Integrating revocation actions with identity and access management systems can further enhance coordination and policy enforcement across the organization.

The design of token expiry and revocation policies must consider user experience alongside security. Systems that enforce aggressive expiry times without proper refresh mechanisms can frustrate users, leading to abandonment or insecure workarounds. On the other hand, excessively long-lived tokens increase the risk of abuse. Configurable policies that adapt based on user roles, behavior, device type, and risk level offer a more balanced solution. For instance, an administrator account may have shorter token lifetimes and stricter revocation policies compared to a regular user accessing low-sensitivity data.

Ultimately, managing token expiry and revocation is not a one-size-fits-all problem. It requires a tailored approach that aligns with the risk profile, architecture, and user requirements of the system. Security teams must define clear guidelines, automate enforcement where possible, and continually assess the effectiveness of their token policies. As threats evolve and systems scale, robust token lifecycle management becomes an indispensable element of API security, safeguarding resources while enabling responsive, user-friendly digital experiences.

# Rate Limiting and Throttling for Abuse Prevention

As APIs become more central to modern applications, platforms, and services, they also become attractive targets for abuse, misuse, and exploitation. To ensure reliability, fairness, and security, it is critical to implement mechanisms that can detect and mitigate excessive or malicious use. Rate limiting and throttling are two of the most effective techniques used to protect APIs from abuse. These mechanisms control how frequently clients can make requests to an API within a specific timeframe, preventing system overload, denial-of-service attacks, data scraping, and other forms of misuse. Their correct implementation not only safeguards resources but also improves user experience by ensuring fair access across clients.

Rate limiting refers to the process of defining a ceiling on the number of requests a client can make in a given time window. For example, an API might allow a maximum of 100 requests per minute per user or 1,000 requests per hour per IP address. If a client exceeds this threshold, subsequent requests are rejected with an appropriate HTTP status code, usually 429 Too Many Requests. This limit is essential for maintaining the stability of backend services, especially in high-traffic environments or when APIs expose computationally expensive operations. Without rate limiting, a single client or group of clients could monopolize system resources, leading to degraded performance or outages for other users.

Throttling, on the other hand, focuses on shaping the flow of incoming requests. Instead of outright rejecting excessive requests, throttling can delay their processing to maintain a consistent load on the server. It acts as a pressure valve, allowing the system to handle bursts of traffic more gracefully without exceeding capacity. Throttling is particularly useful when dealing with services that have dynamic workloads or variable performance characteristics. In many implementations, rate limiting and throttling are used together, where throttling manages short-term spikes and rate limiting enforces long-term usage boundaries.

There are several strategies for implementing rate limiting, each with different trade-offs in terms of accuracy, complexity, and resource consumption. The fixed window algorithm divides time into equal segments and counts the number of requests in each segment. While simple to implement, it suffers from boundary issues where a client can effectively double their allowed rate by timing requests at the edges of two consecutive windows. The sliding window approach provides a more accurate limit by tracking requests in a rolling timeframe, thereby preventing burst abuse. Another common method is the token bucket algorithm, where tokens are added to a bucket at a fixed rate, and each request consumes a token. If no tokens remain, the request is denied. This approach allows for controlled bursts and smooths out traffic over time.

Rate limiting policies can be applied at various levels of granularity. Some systems limit requests based on the user's identity, API key, or OAuth token, ensuring that authenticated users are held accountable for their usage. Others apply limits at the IP address level, which is useful for preventing bot attacks or abuse from anonymous clients. In more advanced scenarios, rate limits can be set per endpoint, per HTTP method, or based on the sensitivity of the data being accessed. This level of customization allows organizations to protect critical services while maintaining accessibility for legitimate users.

Transparency in rate limiting is important for user experience. APIs should communicate their rate limits clearly through documentation and response headers. Headers such as X-RateLimit-Limit, X-RateLimit-Remaining, and X-RateLimit-Reset provide clients with real-time feedback about their usage and help them design systems that adapt gracefully to limits. When a client is rate-limited, the server should include a Retry-After header to indicate when it is safe to try again. This communication helps reduce frustration and encourages developers to build responsible, well-behaved applications.

Abuse prevention is not solely about enforcing static limits. Systems should be designed to detect patterns of abnormal behavior and adapt dynamically. For example, a sudden spike in traffic from a specific IP address or API key could indicate an automated attack or misconfigured script. In such cases, dynamic rate limiting can adjust the thresholds in real time, tightening access for suspicious actors while maintaining normal limits for others. Machine learning and anomaly detection algorithms can further enhance this process by identifying subtle patterns that rule-based systems might miss.

Rate limiting and throttling also play a role in business policy enforcement. For example, different tiers of service in a SaaS platform may come with different rate limits. Free users might have low request limits to prevent abuse and control costs, while enterprise customers may receive higher limits or dedicated API endpoints. This allows organizations to monetize access and scale their infrastructure accordingly. Enforcement of such policies must be consistent and fair, with rate limits applied equally across all instances of a given service tier.

Operational monitoring is essential to validate that rate limiting and throttling mechanisms are working as intended. Metrics such as request rates, rejection counts, average latency, and success ratios should be collected and analyzed in real time. Dashboards and alerts can help detect when limits are being reached too frequently, either due to legitimate growth or abuse. Logs should record when clients exceed limits, including identifying details that aid in troubleshooting or enforcement. Regular audits of rate limiting rules ensure they remain aligned with actual usage patterns and evolving business requirements.

Edge services and API gateways often serve as the first line of defense for implementing rate limiting and throttling. These components can enforce policies before traffic reaches backend services, reducing unnecessary load and improving scalability. Cloud providers and third-party API management platforms also offer built-in support for rate limiting, allowing developers to configure limits declaratively without modifying application code. However, reliance on external services introduces new challenges, such as propagation delays, integration complexity, and dependency management. Balancing centralized control with localized enforcement remains an ongoing design consideration in distributed systems.

Rate limiting and throttling are not purely technical mechanisms; they also serve to enforce trust between API providers and consumers. They encourage responsible usage, protect shared infrastructure, and ensure that one user's behavior does not negatively impact others. As APIs continue to expand in scope and importance, these mechanisms become vital tools in maintaining performance, availability, and fairness. When thoughtfully implemented, rate limiting and throttling do more than protect resources—they build resilience into systems, foster healthy usage patterns, and provide the foundations for scalable, secure API platforms.

# IP Whitelisting and Geofencing Strategies

Controlling access to APIs is a fundamental aspect of building secure systems, and one of the most straightforward and effective ways to enforce this control is through network-based restrictions such as IP whitelisting and geofencing. These techniques serve as outer layers of defense, filtering incoming requests based on the origin of the network traffic before any deeper authentication or authorization logic is applied. While they are not substitutes for identity-based security mechanisms, IP whitelisting and geofencing provide valuable safeguards that can significantly reduce the attack surface, especially when used in conjunction with other controls.

IP whitelisting operates on the principle of allowing traffic only from known, trusted IP addresses or ranges. By explicitly defining which IPs are permitted to access an API, organizations can block all other traffic by default. This strategy is particularly effective in environments where clients have predictable network addresses, such as internal systems, partner integrations, or fixed-location offices. For example, if an internal administration API is only accessed by backend services within a corporate network, the API can be configured to reject requests from any external IP. This eliminates a vast number of potential threats from the public internet and reduces the exposure of sensitive endpoints.

Implementing IP whitelisting can be done at various layers of the application stack. At the network level, firewalls and load balancers can enforce IP restrictions before traffic even reaches the application server. At the application layer, middleware can inspect the client's IP address and reject requests that do not match the allowed list. Cloud-based API gateways often provide built-in support for IP filtering, allowing policies to be configured declaratively. Regardless of where it is enforced, the effectiveness of IP whitelisting depends on maintaining an accurate and up-to-date list of trusted IPs, which can be challenging in dynamic environments.

One common challenge arises when clients use dynamic IP addresses that change frequently, such as mobile users or cloud-based services that do not have static outbound IPs. In such cases, managing the whitelist becomes more complex and error-prone. Overly broad rules may be added to accommodate variability, which can inadvertently weaken security. VPNs and proxy services further complicate matters, as the true client IP may be masked or altered. Organizations must weigh the security benefits of strict IP filtering against the operational overhead and potential disruptions caused by overly restrictive rules.

Geofencing provides another layer of network-based access control by restricting traffic based on geographic location. This is typically achieved by mapping incoming IP addresses to geographic regions using IP geolocation databases. With geofencing, an API can be configured to allow or deny requests from specific countries, regions, or even cities. This is particularly useful in scenarios where the user base is limited to a certain geographic area, or where compliance regulations prohibit data access from certain regions. For example, a healthcare application serving patients in Europe might block API requests originating from outside the European Union to meet GDPR compliance requirements.

Like IP whitelisting, geofencing can be implemented at multiple levels of the infrastructure. Web application firewalls and API gateways are often the most practical places to enforce geofencing rules, as they can intercept requests early in the processing pipeline. Some cloud providers also offer geographic restrictions as part of their access control services, enabling developers to configure geographic policies without writing custom code. However, geolocation accuracy is not absolute. IP databases can be outdated or imprecise, and IP addresses associated with VPNs or anonymizing proxies may obscure the true location of the client. This makes geofencing a useful but imperfect tool, best used as part of a broader security strategy.

There are also important considerations around user experience and accessibility when deploying geofencing. Blocking access based on geography can inadvertently lock out legitimate users who are traveling, using international ISPs, or working remotely from unexpected locations. To address this, systems can provide fallback mechanisms such as manual approval requests or support tickets that allow temporary exceptions. These mechanisms must be carefully managed to prevent abuse while maintaining usability for trusted users.

For both IP whitelisting and geofencing, logging and monitoring play crucial roles in maintaining effectiveness. Every denied request should be logged with metadata such as timestamp, source IP, and geolocation data. These logs provide valuable insights into attempted access patterns and can help identify emerging threats or misconfigurations. They also support forensic investigations in the event of a breach or security incident. Integration with security information and event management (SIEM) systems can further enhance detection and response capabilities by correlating network events with other indicators of compromise.

Maintaining dynamic control over IP whitelists and geofencing rules requires automation. Manual updates are error-prone and often lag behind real-world changes. Organizations should implement systems that allow whitelists to be updated programmatically via APIs or infrastructure-as-code pipelines. For example, when a new partner is onboarded, their IP addresses can be added to the whitelist as part of the deployment process. Likewise, if a threat is detected from a particular region, geofencing rules can be updated in real time to block further access. This agility is essential in defending against fast-moving attacks and adapting to changing operational requirements.

It is also important to recognize that network-based access controls are only part of a comprehensive API security strategy. They work best when combined with robust authentication, authorization, and data protection mechanisms. While IP whitelisting and geofencing can effectively reduce exposure and deter casual attackers, they do not protect against insider threats or compromised devices within the trusted network. Zero trust principles, which assume no implicit trust based on network location, advocate for continuous verification of identity and context. In such models, IP-based controls are just one layer among many that contribute to a defense-in-depth approach.

Despite their limitations, IP whitelisting and geofencing remain valuable tools for securing APIs against unauthorized access. They provide a first line of defense that filters traffic based on origin, reducing the volume of potentially malicious requests and focusing security resources on more sophisticated threats. When implemented with care, kept up to date, and integrated into a broader security framework, these strategies can significantly enhance the resilience and integrity of API-driven systems. As the threat landscape continues to evolve, revisiting and refining network-based access controls will remain an essential part of maintaining a secure and trustworthy API environment.

# CORS Policies and Cross-Origin Access

Cross-Origin Resource Sharing, commonly referred to as CORS, is a critical component of web security and API management. It is a mechanism that defines how resources on a web server can be accessed by web applications running on a different domain. CORS policies are enforced by browsers to prevent malicious scripts on one website from making unauthorized requests to another. While the same-origin policy offers baseline protection by restricting cross-origin HTTP requests, modern applications often require resources to be shared across domains. CORS was developed to provide a secure, standardized way to relax these restrictions when necessary. For APIs, especially those intended for consumption by web applications, understanding and implementing proper CORS policies is essential to maintaining both security and functionality.

When a web application attempts to make an HTTP request to a different domain, protocol, or port from where it originated, the browser performs a CORS check. If the target server does not include the appropriate CORS headers in its response, the browser blocks the request before it reaches the server or before the response is processed by the client. This security measure is particularly important for APIs that expose sensitive data or allow operations that can affect system state. Without CORS, a malicious actor could potentially use a victim's browser to send forged requests to another site where the user is authenticated, leading to data leakage or unauthorized actions.

CORS relies on specific HTTP headers to determine whether a cross-origin request should be allowed. The most fundamental of these is the Access-Control-Allow-Origin header, which specifies which origin or origins are permitted to access the resource. This header can be set to a specific domain, a list of domains, or a wildcard value indicating that all origins are allowed. Using the wildcard is convenient for public APIs that do not handle sensitive information, but it must be avoided for endpoints requiring authentication or handling user data. Allowing all origins without proper control can open the door to cross-site attacks, especially when combined with cookies, tokens, or other credentials.

Another important header is Access-Control-Allow-Methods, which indicates which HTTP methods are permitted when accessing the resource. Common methods include GET, POST, PUT, DELETE, and OPTIONS. Servers must explicitly declare which methods are safe for cross-origin requests. This ensures that applications cannot perform unauthorized actions by exploiting unguarded endpoints. Similarly, the Access-Control-Allow-Headers header lists the custom headers that can be used in the actual request, such as Authorization, Content-Type, or X-Custom-Header. Without this declaration, browsers may block requests that include headers not deemed safe by default.

For some requests, such as those involving non-simple methods or custom headers, browsers perform a preflight request. This preflight is an OPTIONS request sent by the browser before the actual request is made. It is designed to check whether the actual request is safe to send. The server must respond with the appropriate CORS headers, confirming that the intended action is permitted. If the server fails to respond correctly, the browser cancels the request, providing a layer of defense against unintended interactions. This process adds latency to the user experience, so developers often optimize API design to minimize the number of preflight requests.

Credentialed requests introduce another layer of complexity. When a web application needs to include credentials such as cookies or HTTP authentication headers, the CORS policy must explicitly allow them.

This is done using the Access-Control-Allow-Credentials header, which must be set to true. Additionally, the Access-Control-Allow-Origin header cannot use a wildcard in this case; it must specify the exact origin. This restriction helps prevent unauthorized sites from leveraging a user's authenticated session on a different origin. Misconfiguration in this area can lead to serious security vulnerabilities, particularly in systems that rely on session cookies for authentication.

Developers and administrators must exercise caution when configuring CORS headers. A common mistake is allowing too much by default, such as enabling all origins or methods without fully considering the implications. Automated tools or misapplied code snippets can introduce overly permissive CORS policies that defeat the entire purpose of the mechanism. It is crucial to define CORS policies that are as restrictive as possible while still allowing legitimate use cases. Proper testing, validation, and review of CORS configurations should be part of the development and deployment process.

APIs intended for public use, such as open data platforms or content delivery services, may have more lenient CORS policies. In these cases, allowing all origins can be acceptable, provided that the API does not involve user-specific or sensitive data. However, even public APIs should consider throttling, API keys, or other forms of usage control to prevent abuse. For private or internal APIs, or those integrated into enterprise applications, CORS should be tightly controlled, with origin whitelists that are updated and maintained carefully. Logging and monitoring of CORS-related request failures can help identify misconfigurations and potential security issues.

From a development perspective, understanding CORS is essential when building web applications that rely on APIs. Developers frequently encounter CORS errors during development due to mismatches between the frontend and backend environments. These issues can be addressed by configuring development servers to proxy API requests or by adjusting server-side CORS headers appropriately. It is also important for frontend developers to understand the difference between CORS-related failures and actual server errors, as the browser may block responses even when the server returns a valid status.

Emerging architectures such as microservices and single-page applications increase the importance of CORS management. As applications are decomposed into services running on different subdomains or ports, cross-origin requests become more common. Managing CORS policies across multiple services requires a coordinated approach, often supported by API gateways or service meshes that centralize and enforce access control. Consistency is key, as inconsistent CORS behavior can lead to unpredictable failures or security loopholes.

CORS is also evolving as browser vendors and standards bodies respond to new threats and use cases. Enhanced tracking protection, stricter cookie handling rules, and new security headers all intersect with CORS policies. Developers must stay informed about changes in browser behavior and update their configurations accordingly. For instance, recent changes in how cookies are treated in cross-origin requests under the SameSite attribute have implications for applications that rely on session-based authentication in a cross-origin context.

Understanding and implementing secure CORS policies is essential for any API that will be accessed from browsers. It enables controlled, secure sharing of resources while protecting against unauthorized access and malicious activity. While CORS adds complexity to web development, it is a necessary layer in a modern, security-conscious API ecosystem. By treating CORS not just as a technical hurdle but as a strategic control point, organizations can improve both security and reliability in their API offerings.

# Input Validation to Prevent Injection Attacks

Input validation is one of the most essential techniques in securing APIs against injection attacks. These attacks exploit vulnerabilities in the way applications handle untrusted user input, allowing attackers to manipulate backend systems, execute arbitrary commands, or access unauthorized data. Injection attacks can occur in many forms, including SQL injection, command injection, XML injection, and NoSQL injection, among others. In each case, the core issue stems from a failure to properly inspect and sanitize the data that enters the system. By ensuring that all user input is validated before being processed or stored, developers can significantly reduce the risk of these attacks and preserve the integrity of their applications.

APIs, by their nature, are interfaces designed to accept input and deliver responses. Whether an API is receiving a search term, a username, a JSON payload, or query parameters, it is essentially processing user-provided data. When this data is not properly validated, it becomes a vector through which malicious payloads can be injected. For example, in a SQL injection attack, an attacker might insert SQL commands into a text input field or URL parameter, tricking the API into executing them against the database. If the input is passed directly into a SQL query without validation or parameterization, the consequences can be devastating, ranging from data leaks to full database compromise.

The foundation of effective input validation is the principle of whitelisting rather than blacklisting. This means defining exactly what kind of input is acceptable, and rejecting everything else. For instance, if an API expects a username that contains only alphanumeric characters and is between five and twenty characters long, it should enforce those rules strictly. Input that falls outside these boundaries should be immediately rejected. This approach ensures that only well-formed, expected data reaches the processing layer, reducing the likelihood that an attacker can sneak malicious content through the cracks.

Validation should be applied at multiple levels. It begins at the client side, where front-end applications can enforce basic input constraints such as field length, allowed characters, or format patterns. However, client-side validation can never be trusted alone, since it is easily bypassed using tools like Postman, curl, or custom scripts. Therefore, robust validation must always occur server-side, where the API can make authoritative decisions about what input is allowed. At the server, developers can implement schema validation for structured inputs such as JSON or XML. Schema validation tools allow developers to define precise expectations for incoming payloads, including required fields, data types, formats, and nested object structures.

Sanitization is another crucial part of the input validation process. While validation ensures that input is well-formed and appropriate, sanitization modifies the input to remove or neutralize harmful elements. For example, if an API accepts HTML content for a user bio field, it must sanitize the input to strip out potentially dangerous tags or attributes that could be used in a cross-site scripting attack. Similarly, if user input is displayed in a webpage, it must be properly escaped to prevent script execution. APIs that serve as backends to web applications must pay special attention to these issues, as improperly sanitized output can turn even harmless-looking input into an active threat.

Parameterized queries, also known as prepared statements, are one of the most effective defenses against SQL injection attacks. Rather than concatenating user input directly into SQL strings, parameterized queries use placeholders for data and bind the actual values later. This approach ensures that user input is treated as data rather than executable code, preventing attackers from injecting malicious SQL commands. Most modern database libraries and ORM frameworks support parameterized queries out of the box, and developers should adopt them consistently across all database operations. The same principle applies to other technologies as well, including command-line execution, XML parsing, and NoSQL queries.

APIs that integrate with third-party systems or external services must also validate the input they send and receive. Just as unvalidated input from users can be dangerous, so too can malformed or malicious data from partner systems. This is particularly relevant in microservice architectures, where one API may rely on the output of another. In these cases, contracts and schemas should be defined clearly, and validation should be applied to both incoming and outgoing data. Trust boundaries must be established and enforced, with strict controls around data formats, expected values, and error handling.

Logging and monitoring play an important role in the overall strategy of input validation. When invalid input is detected, it should be logged with sufficient detail to allow for analysis, but without exposing sensitive information such as tokens, credentials, or personal data. Patterns in rejected input can indicate automated scanning, brute-force attempts, or targeted attacks. Monitoring tools can use this data to alert administrators, block abusive IP addresses, or trigger defensive actions such as rate limiting or CAPTCHA challenges. Input validation is not just a technical measure but also an important source of security intelligence.

One of the most overlooked aspects of input validation is consistency. In large applications, different developers or teams may apply different validation rules to similar inputs, creating inconsistencies that attackers can exploit. For example, if one endpoint validates email addresses strictly while another does not, an attacker might use the weaker endpoint to inject payloads or circumvent business logic. To prevent this, organizations should define a centralized validation strategy and provide shared libraries or middleware that enforce consistent rules across all APIs. These components should be maintained alongside the application and tested rigorously to ensure correctness.

Validation must also be adaptable. As applications evolve, so do the types of input they accept. New features may introduce new data types, optional fields, or complex structures. Security teams and developers must review validation rules regularly to ensure they remain aligned with current requirements. Outdated rules can either allow new forms of attack or cause legitimate requests to fail unexpectedly. Automated testing can help identify discrepancies and ensure that validation logic performs as expected across a wide range of inputs.

Securing APIs against injection attacks starts with a deep commitment to input validation. By rejecting invalid or unexpected input, sanitizing user-provided data, and consistently applying validation logic across all layers of the application, developers can eliminate many of the entry points attackers rely on. Input validation is not glamorous, and it may seem like a basic task, but its importance in the defense of APIs cannot be overstated. In a world where data flows between countless users, systems, and services, the ability to say no to malicious input is one of the most powerful tools available to API developers and security professionals.

# Output Encoding and Response Sanitization

Securing APIs involves not only controlling and validating the data that enters a system but also carefully managing the data that exits it. Output encoding and response sanitization are essential techniques used to prevent the delivery of malicious or unintended content through API responses. These techniques play a critical role in defending against client-side attacks, particularly cross-site scripting (XSS), content injection, and data leakage. In modern application architectures, APIs often serve as the backend for web, mobile, and third-party clients, meaning any unsanitized or improperly encoded data delivered through an API could be directly rendered in a user's browser or displayed in a user interface. Attackers frequently exploit these opportunities to execute scripts, hijack sessions, exfiltrate data, or perform other harmful actions. Therefore, ensuring that API responses are clean, well-structured, and safe to consume is a non-negotiable part of API security.

Output encoding is the process of converting potentially dangerous characters into a safe format before they are included in a response. This is especially important when user-supplied input or dynamic data is incorporated into content that will be rendered by a client application, such as a web page. Characters like the less-than sign, greater-than sign, ampersand, and quotation marks can be interpreted as part of HTML, JavaScript, or other markup languages. If not encoded properly, these characters can alter the behavior of the client application or inject executable code into the browser. Output encoding ensures that such characters are displayed as plain text rather than being parsed as executable instructions. For example, encoding a less-than symbol as &lt; prevents the browser from interpreting it as the start of an HTML tag.

In the context of APIs, output encoding is particularly important when generating responses that may be rendered in HTML, embedded in JavaScript, or included in attributes or URLs. Each of these contexts requires a specific type of encoding. HTML encoding is used to protect content inserted into HTML documents. JavaScript encoding protects content embedded within scripts. URL encoding ensures that data included in URLs is interpreted correctly and does not alter the structure of the URL itself. Developers must be aware of the context in which data will be used and apply the appropriate encoding technique accordingly. Encoding content for the wrong context, or failing to encode it at all, can leave the application vulnerable to code injection and data manipulation.

Response sanitization goes hand in hand with output encoding but serves a slightly different purpose. While encoding transforms dangerous content into a safe format, sanitization involves removing or neutralizing undesirable content altogether. This is often necessary when APIs return content submitted by users, such as comments, form inputs, or uploaded files. Sanitization tools can strip out HTML tags, remove embedded scripts, disallow specific attributes, or clean up malformed content. This ensures that the data returned by the API does not include executable code or other harmful payloads that could compromise the client environment.

APIs that support rich content inputs must be particularly careful in how they sanitize outputs. For instance, a blogging platform may allow users to submit HTML-formatted posts. In such a case, the API cannot simply strip all tags, but must instead allow a safe subset of tags and attributes while blocking those that could be used for scripting or layout manipulation. Libraries like DOMPurify and OWASP Java HTML Sanitizer are widely used for this purpose. They provide configurable options to define allowed tags, attributes, and CSS styles while ensuring the resulting HTML is safe to render. Implementing these libraries on the server side before returning content through an API helps prevent the distribution of malicious or unsafe HTML.

Another important aspect of response sanitization is data exposure control. APIs must ensure that they do not inadvertently include sensitive or internal fields in their responses. This can happen when objects are serialized directly from internal data structures without filtering. Fields like passwords, internal IDs, debug flags, or backend configuration settings should never appear in API responses. Developers must define explicit response models or view serializers that include only the necessary and safe fields. This principle, known as output whitelisting, ensures that only intended data is exposed and reduces the risk of accidental leaks.

Error messages and stack traces are another common source of unintended data exposure. When APIs encounter exceptions or fail to process requests correctly, they often return error responses. If these responses include verbose messages, database query fragments, or exception stack traces, they may provide attackers with valuable insights into the underlying system. Proper response sanitization includes customizing error messages to be informative but not revealing. Instead of exposing internal implementation details, APIs should use standardized error codes, generic messages, and logs for internal debugging purposes.

Content-type headers and response formats also play a role in output safety. APIs must ensure that they declare and enforce the correct content type for their responses. For example, if an API returns a JSON object, it should include a Content-Type: application/json header. Failure to set this header correctly could result in browsers interpreting the content in unintended ways, potentially leading to script execution. For text-based responses such as HTML or plain text, additional security headers like X-Content-Type-Options: nosniff can help prevent content-type guessing and further protect against injection attacks.

Output encoding and sanitization are not one-time efforts but ongoing responsibilities. As APIs evolve, new endpoints, data structures, and rendering contexts are introduced. Developers must continuously assess how data flows through the system and update encoding and sanitization logic as needed. Automated testing can help catch issues before they reach production. Security testing tools, both static and dynamic, can scan API responses for patterns indicative of injection risks or unencoded user input. Security reviews and code audits provide another layer of assurance, helping to identify areas where responses may not be adequately protected.

APIs that return structured formats such as JSON, XML, or YAML are not immune to injection attacks. In some cases, user-supplied values may be inserted into these formats in ways that affect client-side parsing or execution. XML injection, JSONP-based cross-site scripting, and template injection are examples of attacks that can exploit unsafe output even in seemingly safe formats. Developers must apply the same diligence to these formats as they would to HTML or script content. Wherever user-controlled input is incorporated into an output structure, it must be carefully inspected, encoded, or sanitized to ensure that it cannot break the intended format or introduce executable behavior.

The role of output encoding and response sanitization is central to maintaining API trustworthiness. While input validation is the first line of defense against malicious data entering the system, output protection ensures that nothing dangerous leaves the system. APIs are conduits of data, and the data they return is often passed along to other systems, components, or user interfaces. Any weakness in how this data is presented or formatted can have ripple effects that compromise security at multiple levels. A disciplined approach to output encoding and sanitization allows developers to create robust, reliable, and secure APIs that can safely serve users across a wide variety of contexts and use cases.

# Protecting Against Cross-Site Scripting in APIs

Cross-Site Scripting, commonly known as XSS, remains one of the most persistent and dangerous vulnerabilities in web security, and APIs play a significant role in either mitigating or enabling this threat. While XSS is traditionally associated with websites and browser-based applications, APIs are increasingly targeted because they serve as conduits for data exchange between clients and servers. APIs that process user input or generate dynamic content can inadvertently become vehicles for XSS payloads if the data they return is not properly validated, sanitized, and encoded. As web and mobile applications rely heavily on APIs for their functionality, protecting against XSS in this context has become an essential aspect of secure API design.

XSS occurs when untrusted input is included in a web page or application output without proper sanitization or encoding, allowing an attacker to execute malicious scripts in the victim's browser. In the case of APIs, the risk emerges when the API accepts user-provided input and returns it in a format that may eventually be rendered in an HTML context by the consuming client. This is common in modern single-page applications that retrieve data via RESTful APIs and dynamically update the DOM using JavaScript frameworks. If the API returns unsanitized user input, and the frontend blindly injects it into the page without proper context-aware encoding, a simple message or comment submitted by a user could become a vector for injecting JavaScript code.

Protecting APIs against XSS starts with understanding that any data returned by an API might be rendered on a client somewhere. Therefore, the first line of defense is input validation. Although input validation alone cannot stop XSS, it helps prevent obvious attacks by restricting the types and formats of input that are allowed. This includes setting constraints on length, structure, and character sets. For instance, an input field expected to contain a user's name should not allow script tags or special characters associated with JavaScript execution. Still, validation is not enough on its own because it cannot account for every possible XSS payload, especially those designed to evade common filters.

The next critical defense is output encoding. When an API delivers content that might be displayed in a browser, it must ensure that any embedded user input is safely encoded for the intended context. If data is inserted into an HTML body, it should be HTML-encoded. If it appears inside a JavaScript block, it must be JavaScript-encoded. The same applies to attributes, CSS, and URLs. Output encoding transforms potentially dangerous characters, such as less-than signs, quotation marks, or ampersands, into harmless equivalents that the browser renders as text rather than interpreting them as code. This technique is particularly effective when consistently applied at the point of output, just before data is rendered by the client.

Many APIs return structured formats such as JSON, which are not inherently dangerous. However, the danger arises when these JSON responses are consumed by frontend code that dynamically injects values into the DOM. A common mistake is taking values from an API and inserting them directly into innerHTML properties or similar

DOM APIs without sanitization. Even if the API returns clean JSON, the frontend's rendering logic can introduce vulnerabilities if it fails to properly encode or sanitize content before display. This means that both the API and the client share responsibility for preventing XSS, and secure development practices must be enforced across both layers.

APIs must also be cautious when supporting features that allow rich content input, such as markdown or HTML formatting. If an API allows users to submit HTML content, as is common in comment systems, blog posts, or content management platforms, it must employ a rigorous sanitization process. This involves stripping or neutralizing dangerous elements like script tags, event handlers, and JavaScript URLs. Specialized libraries exist for this purpose, allowing developers to define safe HTML policies that whitelist permitted tags and attributes. Sanitizing user input before storing or returning it is critical in preventing stored XSS, where malicious code is saved in a database and served to multiple users through subsequent API responses.

Content security policies (CSPs) are a powerful browser-side defense that can help mitigate XSS by controlling which scripts are allowed to execute. While CSPs are implemented on the client side via HTTP headers, APIs can support their enforcement by ensuring responses include appropriate CSP headers when serving content. For APIs that are tightly integrated with frontend applications, setting a restrictive CSP can block inline scripts, prevent loading from untrusted sources, and reduce the impact of any successful XSS attempts. Combining CSP with strict output sanitization and encoding provides a robust multi-layered defense against XSS.

Authentication and session management also play an indirect but important role in XSS protection. If an attacker successfully injects a script via an API response and that script executes in a logged-in user's browser, it can access cookies, tokens, or session data, leading to session hijacking. APIs that use cookies for authentication should set flags like HttpOnly and Secure to prevent client-side access and enforce transmission over HTTPS. In token-based authentication models, such as those using JSON Web Tokens, proper token storage practices are essential. Storing tokens in HTTP-only cookies instead of localStorage or sessionStorage reduces the risk of token theft through XSS.

Monitoring and logging are important for detecting and responding to XSS attempts. APIs should log suspicious input, such as attempts to inject script tags or obfuscated JavaScript payloads. This data can be analyzed to identify attack patterns, trace abuse back to specific IPs or accounts, and improve validation and sanitization logic. Additionally, security testing tools, both static and dynamic, should be used during development and deployment to scan for XSS vulnerabilities. Penetration testing and code reviews focusing on data flow from input to output can help identify gaps in protection before they are exploited in production environments.

Cross-site scripting is often thought of as a frontend vulnerability, but in modern application ecosystems where APIs drive the exchange of content between systems, the API is an integral part of the attack surface. Secure APIs must be designed with the assumption that any user input could be malicious and any response might be rendered in a sensitive context. By validating input, encoding output, sanitizing responses, enforcing security headers, and working in concert with frontend logic, APIs can be hardened against one of the most pervasive and damaging classes of web vulnerabilities. Developers and security professionals must maintain constant vigilance and apply layered defenses to keep applications and users safe from the evolving threat of cross-site scripting.

# Mitigating Cross-Site Request Forgery in APIs

Cross-Site Request Forgery, or CSRF, is a class of web vulnerability that tricks authenticated users into unknowingly performing actions on a system they are logged into, using their active session. It relies on the assumption that the user's browser automatically includes authentication credentials such as cookies or headers when making a request to a target site. In the context of APIs, CSRF is a serious concern when authentication mechanisms involve browser-managed credentials and when the API is capable of performing state-changing operations such as creating, updating, or deleting data. Mitigating CSRF in APIs requires an understanding of how requests are authenticated, how user sessions are managed, and how attackers attempt to exploit implicit trust in those sessions.

Traditionally, CSRF has been more closely associated with web applications, where attackers might craft malicious links or hidden forms that submit requests to vulnerable endpoints. However, as APIs have become more tightly coupled with frontend applications through technologies like AJAX and single-page application frameworks, the risk of CSRF has extended to backend services and APIs that interact with them. If an API is consumed by a frontend that uses browser cookies for authentication, and if that API accepts cross-origin requests that change data or perform sensitive operations, it is potentially vulnerable to CSRF. This risk is exacerbated when the API responds to GET requests by performing state changes, fails to validate request origin, or lacks appropriate protection mechanisms.

One of the foundational strategies for mitigating CSRF in APIs is enforcing the use of stateless authentication mechanisms that do not rely on browser-managed cookies. Token-based authentication schemes, such as those using Bearer tokens in the Authorization header, do not suffer from the same automatic inclusion behavior as cookies. Since tokens must be explicitly attached to each request by the client, the browser cannot be tricked into submitting a token on behalf of the user unless that token has already been compromised. This explicitness disrupts the assumptions on which CSRF attacks are built and forms the basis for safer API interaction models. APIs that adopt JSON Web Tokens (JWT) or OAuth 2.0 access tokens should avoid placing them in storage mechanisms like localStorage that are accessible to JavaScript unless combined with protections against cross-site scripting.

For APIs that still rely on session cookies or other credentials automatically included by the browser, additional CSRF defenses must be implemented. One of the most effective protections is the use of CSRF tokens. These are randomly generated, single-use tokens that are embedded into forms or client-side requests and validated by the server on receipt. Because the attacker cannot read the content of the target site due to the same-origin policy, they cannot obtain a valid CSRF token. Thus, any forged request will be rejected by the server for lacking a valid token. CSRF tokens should be unpredictable, associated with the user's session, and expire after a short time. APIs that use frameworks supporting cookie-based sessions should enable and configure CSRF token support to cover all endpoints that accept state-changing operations.

In addition to token-based defenses, APIs can be protected by validating the origin of incoming requests. This involves checking the Origin and Referer headers sent by the browser with each request. These headers indicate the source of the request and can be used to detect whether the request originated from a trusted site. If the origin does not match an allowed domain, the server can reject the request before it is processed. While the Referer header can be stripped or manipulated by some clients or intermediaries, the Origin header is generally more reliable and consistent for this type of validation. Implementing origin checks adds a valuable layer of defense, particularly for applications that support cross-origin interaction through web browsers.

SameSite cookie attributes also provide significant protection against CSRF. The SameSite attribute instructs the browser when cookies should be included with cross-site requests. When set to Strict, cookies are never included on requests originating from a different site. When set to Lax, cookies are included only on top-level navigation requests using safe methods like GET. When set to None, cookies are included in all cross-site requests but must be marked as Secure. By configuring SameSite correctly, developers can prevent the browser from sending session cookies in scenarios where a CSRF attack might be attempted. Most modern browsers now enforce stricter defaults around SameSite cookies, making them a more reliable component of CSRF mitigation.

It is also important to adopt a least-privilege approach to API permissions and access control. Even if an attacker successfully submits a forged request, the impact can be minimized if the authenticated user lacks the permissions to perform high-risk operations. APIs should segment access based on roles, enforce authorization checks at every endpoint, and log suspicious or anomalous behavior. Limiting what each token or session is allowed to do ensures that even in the event of partial compromise, the damage is contained. Combined with strong authentication practices and CSRF-specific defenses, this approach strengthens the overall resilience of the API.

CSRF prevention is not limited to server-side logic. Frontend applications have a role to play in ensuring secure API interaction. Single-page applications should avoid submitting sensitive requests automatically, especially upon page load or without user interaction. User intent should be required for actions that result in data modification. Additionally, frontend developers should avoid exposing authentication tokens in vulnerable storage locations and should ensure that all requests requiring authentication include the appropriate headers and metadata. Cooperation between frontend and backend development teams is essential to implement and maintain CSRF protections effectively.

Security testing is critical to verifying that APIs are adequately protected against CSRF. Automated tools can simulate CSRF scenarios by attempting to submit unauthorized requests using forged credentials. These tests should be part of the continuous integration pipeline and should cover all endpoints that modify data or trigger transactions. Manual testing, including penetration testing by skilled professionals, can uncover more subtle vulnerabilities, such as improperly scoped tokens, missing origin checks, or endpoints that bypass CSRF verification. Security reviews and code audits further reinforce the process by identifying design patterns or configurations that may introduce risk.

APIs must be designed with the assumption that they are always under scrutiny and that every endpoint could be the target of a CSRF attempt. By moving away from implicit trust models and toward explicit, verifiable request mechanisms, developers can neutralize the underlying assumptions that make CSRF possible. Whether through the adoption of stateless authentication, the use of anti-CSRF tokens, the enforcement of same-origin policies, or careful session configuration, defending against CSRF in APIs requires layered, intentional, and continuously reviewed safeguards. As API ecosystems grow in complexity and integration with frontend systems deepens, the demand for robust CSRF protection only increases, making it a permanent fixture in the landscape of secure application design.

# Handling Sensitive Data in API Requests

APIs frequently serve as the communication backbone for applications that deal with sensitive data, including personally identifiable information, financial records, authentication credentials, and health-related content. Because APIs are often exposed to the internet, used by multiple clients, and integrated into diverse environments, the way they handle sensitive data must be designed with extreme care. Poor practices in transmitting, processing, or storing sensitive information can lead to devastating security breaches, loss of customer trust, and serious legal repercussions. Securing sensitive data in API requests requires a multi-layered approach that spans encryption, access control, input validation, response sanitization, and comprehensive logging policies, all applied with the assumption that every request could be an attack vector.

The first and most fundamental rule in handling sensitive data in API requests is to ensure that all communication is encrypted in transit. This means enforcing HTTPS for every request, without exception. Sensitive data must never be sent over unencrypted channels, even within internal networks or development environments. Modern TLS protocols provide confidentiality and integrity, ensuring that intercepted data cannot be read or altered by attackers. APIs should be configured to redirect HTTP requests to HTTPS, use strong ciphers, and maintain current certificates signed by trusted authorities. Enforcing HTTP Strict Transport Security headers adds another layer by instructing clients to always use HTTPS for future communications.

Beyond transmission security, APIs must carefully manage what kinds of sensitive data they accept and how that data is structured. Sensitive fields should be clearly defined and limited to only what is necessary for the intended function. Collecting excess personal or confidential information increases the risk surface and complicates compliance with regulations such as GDPR or HIPAA. Every request payload should be designed to minimize the inclusion of sensitive elements, especially for endpoints that do not need them. When sensitive data is required, such as in authentication, user registration, or financial transactions, the API should expect it in tightly controlled formats and use strict validation to reject malformed or suspicious input.

Authentication credentials, such as passwords, access tokens, and API keys, are among the most frequently transmitted forms of sensitive data. APIs must ensure that passwords are never stored or logged in plain text, and that they are never exposed in URLs, as query parameters can be logged by intermediaries or appear in browser history. Credentials should always be sent in the request body or headers, protected by HTTPS, and processed immediately using secure hashing algorithms where applicable. Access tokens and keys must be short-lived when possible, scoped to the minimum required permissions, and stored securely on the client. Server-side systems must also protect stored secrets by encrypting them at rest using robust, hardware backed encryption strategies.

Data classification plays a crucial role in how sensitive information is handled. Not all data has the same level of sensitivity, and APIs should distinguish between public, internal, confidential, and highly restricted data types. These classifications can guide policies for data handling, such as how long data is retained, where it can be logged, whether it must be encrypted at rest, and who is authorized to access it. Data classified as highly sensitive should never be returned in full in API responses, logged to files, or cached unless those systems are equally secured. APIs should avoid echoing sensitive data back in error messages, even if the input is invalid, as this can provide attackers with clues about the system's behavior or structure.

Input validation is essential for ensuring that sensitive data received by an API has not been tampered with or manipulated to exploit the system. All incoming data should be validated not only for correct format but also for content that aligns with business logic. For example, an API should not only check that a social security number is composed of nine digits but also verify that it follows a valid issuance pattern or exists in the expected database. This kind of validation helps prevent not just input errors but also potential fraud. Additionally, APIs should enforce rate limiting and throttling to prevent brute-force attempts to guess sensitive data, such as account numbers or authentication codes.

Sensitive data often must be stored temporarily or persistently after it is received by the API. In such cases, encryption at rest is mandatory. Databases, file systems, and logs that store sensitive data must use strong encryption keys, managed securely through key management systems. Access to encrypted data must be strictly controlled and monitored. Systems should enforce the principle of least privilege, ensuring that only specific services or users can decrypt or access sensitive content. For highly sensitive data, such as biometric identifiers or financial account numbers, additional protections such as tokenization or split key storage may be appropriate.

Another area that requires careful attention is API logging. While logging is essential for monitoring, debugging, and auditing, it must be done in a way that does not expose sensitive information. Log entries should be scrubbed of passwords, authentication tokens, and personally identifiable information. Masking or redacting sensitive fields in logs helps prevent accidental disclosure through log access or analysis tools. Logging infrastructure must be protected with access controls, and retention policies should be applied to ensure that logs containing sensitive data do not persist longer than necessary. Security audits should regularly verify that sensitive data is not present in logs and that logging policies are aligned with industry best practices.

Access control is another pillar of securely handling sensitive data in API requests. Not all users or systems should have access to every piece of data. Role-based access control, attribute-based access control, or policy-based access control mechanisms should be applied to restrict who can send or retrieve sensitive data via API endpoints. Each request should be evaluated not just on whether the requester is authenticated, but also whether they are authorized to access the specific data or operation. Fine-grained permissions help prevent data leakage from compromised accounts or misconfigured clients.

Security monitoring and auditing must be continuous. Systems should track access to sensitive data, including when it was accessed, by whom, and for what purpose. This level of visibility is critical not only for breach detection but also for compliance with regulatory standards. APIs should emit security-related events, such as unauthorized access attempts or abnormal data patterns, to centralized monitoring systems. Automated alerts can trigger incident response processes, enabling rapid action when suspicious activity is detected.

Educating developers and stakeholders is essential to ensure that everyone handling sensitive data understands the implications of their design and coding decisions. Secure coding practices, data protection policies, and threat awareness should be part of regular training. Security should not be left to post-development audits; it must be built into the development lifecycle from the first design meetings to the final deployment pipeline.

Handling sensitive data in API requests is a continuous responsibility that demands precision, awareness, and a deep respect for user privacy and system security. Every line of code that accepts or processes sensitive data must be crafted with the understanding that a single misstep can have far-reaching consequences. By encrypting communication, validating and sanitizing input, controlling access, minimizing exposure, and applying strong operational controls, developers and security teams can ensure that APIs remain a trusted and secure bridge between users and the systems that serve them.

# Securing Data in Transit with HTTPS

The transmission of data across networks, especially the public internet, is one of the most vulnerable moments in the lifecycle of digital information. APIs, by their nature, are conduits for transmitting data between clients and servers, and often this data is sensitive, including personal identifiers, credentials, financial records, and proprietary information. If these transmissions are not adequately protected, attackers can intercept, view, or modify the data, leading to privacy breaches, credential theft, or system compromise. The standard and most effective solution to secure data in transit is the use of HTTPS, or Hypertext Transfer Protocol Secure. HTTPS encrypts communications using the Transport Layer Security protocol, ensuring that data sent between the client and server remains confidential, unaltered, and authenticated. Implementing HTTPS correctly is not optional; it is a fundamental requirement for any modern API.

HTTPS works by establishing a secure channel between two communicating parties. This process begins with a TLS handshake, during which the client and server agree on encryption algorithms and keys to use for the session. The server presents a digital certificate, issued by a trusted certificate authority, to prove its identity. Once the handshake is complete and trust is established, all further communication is encrypted using symmetric encryption, which is fast and efficient for large volumes of data. This encryption prevents eavesdropping and tampering, as any unauthorized party intercepting the traffic would see only ciphertext that is computationally infeasible to decrypt without the session key.

For APIs, enforcing HTTPS is critical not only for protecting data but also for establishing trust with clients. Browsers and modern HTTP clients have increasingly strict policies regarding HTTPS. Many APIs use authentication tokens, API keys, or session cookies, all of which are vulnerable if transmitted over insecure channels. An attacker who captures these credentials over plain HTTP can impersonate users or gain unauthorized access to systems. Therefore, APIs must be configured to redirect all HTTP requests to HTTPS and refuse to process requests sent over insecure connections. HSTS, or HTTP Strict Transport Security, should also be enabled to instruct browsers to always use HTTPS for future requests to the domain.

Configuring HTTPS for an API begins with obtaining a valid TLS certificate from a reputable certificate authority. This certificate must match the domain name of the API and should be renewed before it expires. Let's Encrypt and other automated certificate authorities make it easier for developers to obtain and renew certificates at no cost. Once installed on the server, the certificate must be configured with strong cipher suites and protocol versions. Deprecated versions of TLS, such as TLS 1.0 and TLS 1.1, should be disabled, and modern, secure versions like TLS 1.2 and TLS 1.3 should be enforced. Cipher suites that offer forward secrecy, which ensures that session keys cannot be derived from a long-term private key, should be prioritized in the server configuration.

The protection of data in transit is not limited to external API calls. Internal APIs used for service-to-service communication must also be secured with HTTPS. In cloud-native architectures and microservices environments, services often communicate with each other across different nodes or containers. These internal networks are not immune to attacks, especially in shared or multi-tenant environments. If an attacker gains access to one node, they may be able to sniff traffic destined for other services if encryption is not enforced. By requiring HTTPS even for internal traffic, organizations can maintain a consistent security posture and prevent lateral movement by attackers within the network.

Another important aspect of securing data in transit is client validation. In a standard HTTPS setup, only the client verifies the identity of the server. In more secure environments, mutual TLS (mTLS) can be used to require the client to present a certificate as well. This ensures that the server only accepts connections from trusted clients, adding a strong layer of authentication to the transport layer. Mutual TLS is particularly effective in APIs used for internal service communication, business-to-business integrations, or any environment where high assurance of client identity is required. Configuring mTLS requires careful management of client certificates, including issuance, rotation, and revocation, which must be handled through a secure and scalable certificate management system.

Monitoring and auditing play an important role in maintaining the security of HTTPS-enabled APIs. TLS handshake failures, certificate errors, or sudden changes in cipher usage can indicate misconfigurations or active attacks such as downgrade attempts or man-in-the-middle scenarios. API gateways, reverse proxies, and monitoring tools should be configured to log and alert on such anomalies. Certificate transparency logs should be checked regularly to ensure no unauthorized certificates have been issued for API domains. Security teams must be vigilant in tracking and responding to any indicators that suggest a breach or attempted compromise of the secure transport layer.

While HTTPS secures the transport channel, it does not encrypt the data once it reaches the server or the client. This means that sensitive data must still be protected at rest and in memory. Logging systems, caching layers, and downstream services must treat decrypted data with the same level of caution. Developers should avoid logging sensitive information, such as passwords or tokens, and ensure that secure memory handling practices are used for processing decrypted data. Additionally, headers such as Cache-Control: no-store and Pragma: no-cache should be used to prevent sensitive data from being cached by browsers or intermediaries.

In complex deployments involving load balancers or content delivery networks, it is essential to terminate TLS connections in a secure manner. Some architectures terminate HTTPS at the edge and forward traffic internally over HTTP. This practice introduces risk if the internal network is not fully trusted or segmented. Instead, TLS should either be terminated at the API server itself or re-encrypted before forwarding. End-to-end encryption ensures that no intermediate system can access the unencrypted payload unless it is specifically authorized and secured to do so.

Securing data in transit with HTTPS is a foundational requirement for protecting API integrity, confidentiality, and trustworthiness. It ensures that information cannot be intercepted or altered by unauthorized entities, enables strong client-server authentication, and serves as the first line of defense against a wide range of network-based attacks. Proper HTTPS implementation is not simply a configuration task; it is a continuous responsibility that requires attention to certificate lifecycle management, protocol updates, encryption strength, and operational monitoring. As APIs continue to power critical applications across industries, the importance of securing every byte of data in transit remains as vital as ever.

# Securing Data at Rest for API Storage

Securing data at rest is a critical component of API security that ensures sensitive information remains protected even when it is stored on persistent media such as databases, file systems, or backup storage. When APIs handle confidential or regulated data—such as user credentials, personal identifiers, financial records, or intellectual property—they bear the responsibility of safeguarding that data not only in transit but also while it resides within the system. Breaches that involve stored data can have severe consequences, including identity theft, regulatory fines, operational disruption, and long-term reputational damage. Effective data-at-rest security requires a combination of encryption, access control, secure architecture, and monitoring, all tailored to the specific requirements and threats associated with the data being stored.

Encryption is the cornerstone of protecting data at rest. It transforms readable data into an unreadable format that can only be decrypted using a specific cryptographic key. For APIs that interact with data stores, encryption must be applied to all sensitive fields and files before they are written to disk. This includes not just structured data in databases but also unstructured data such as uploaded files, logs, or cached content. Strong encryption algorithms like AES-256 should be used, and encryption keys must be managed securely through centralized key management systems. The security of encrypted data is only as strong as the protection of the keys, so these systems should include mechanisms for key rotation, access auditing, and secure storage in hardware security modules or cloud-native key vaults.

Access control is another fundamental layer of securing data at rest. Not all users or services should have unrestricted access to stored data. Access should be governed by the principle of least privilege, meaning each identity—whether a human user or an automated process—should only have access to the specific data needed to perform its function. APIs should use identity and access management systems to define roles and policies that restrict access to encrypted storage or database records. Database credentials, file access permissions, and API configurations must be managed with tight controls and regularly audited to ensure they do not allow excessive or unnecessary access to stored information.

Data minimization complements access control by ensuring that only necessary data is collected and stored. APIs should be designed to accept and retain only the fields essential for their operation. Collecting extra data increases the risk surface and complicates storage requirements. Retention policies should define how long different types of data are kept and when they must be deleted or anonymized. Automating data deletion or expiration ensures that stale data does not linger in storage systems where it can become a liability. Regulatory standards like GDPR, HIPAA, and PCI DSS often mandate specific requirements for data retention and destruction, making compliance a critical consideration in data-at-rest security strategies.

Storage architecture plays a significant role in the security of data at rest. Data should be logically segmented according to sensitivity, with separate storage mechanisms for high-risk and low-risk data. For example, personally identifiable information should not be stored alongside log files or metrics data. Isolating storage reduces the risk that a compromise of one system will expose unrelated sensitive data. APIs should also avoid storing sensitive data in temporary files, local cache directories, or development environments. Every location where data is stored must be subject to the same security policies and protective controls. In cloud environments, APIs should leverage managed storage services that include built-in encryption and security compliance, while still enforcing application-level encryption and access rules.

Audit logging provides visibility into who accesses data and when. Systems should record every access attempt to stored data, whether successful or denied. These logs should include details such as the identity performing the operation, the data accessed, the time of the access, and the action taken. Logs must be protected against tampering and stored in a secure location with strict access controls. Regular review of audit logs is essential for detecting suspicious behavior, identifying misconfigurations, and demonstrating compliance with internal policies and external regulations. When a security incident occurs, detailed audit logs are often the key to understanding the scope and method of the breach.

API designs must also consider the risks of indirect exposure of stored data. Information returned by the API in response to user queries should be limited to only what is necessary. If an API allows querying of a user profile, it should not return sensitive fields like passwords, social security numbers, or internal identifiers unless absolutely required. These fields should be masked, redacted, or omitted entirely. Protecting data at rest includes not only preventing unauthorized access but also ensuring that data is not inadvertently leaked through legitimate channels due to overexposure or insufficient output filtering.

Secure backup practices are vital to any data-at-rest protection plan. Backups must be encrypted, stored securely, and protected with the same level of access control as primary storage systems. APIs that rely on automated backups should ensure that backup files do not contain unencrypted sensitive data or credentials. Backup files must be versioned, integrity-checked, and stored in geographically distributed locations to support disaster recovery while minimizing the risk of centralized compromise. Regular testing of backup restoration processes is critical to ensure that encrypted backups can be successfully decrypted and used when needed, without losing data due to key mismanagement or format corruption.

One area of concern is the handling of stored credentials. APIs that manage user accounts must never store plaintext passwords. Instead, passwords should be hashed using secure, slow hashing algorithms such as bcrypt, scrypt, or Argon2. These algorithms are resistant to brute-force attacks and make it computationally expensive to reverse-engineer passwords from hash values. Even when using such algorithms, additional protections like salting each password and enforcing strong password policies help ensure that stored credentials are resilient against attack. Similarly, tokens, API keys, and other authentication secrets must be stored in a way that prevents unauthorized retrieval or misuse, preferably with one-way encryption or secure wrapping techniques.

Data-at-rest security must also be integrated into the software development lifecycle. Secure storage practices should be enforced through code reviews, automated tests, and deployment pipelines. Developers must be trained to recognize the importance of secure data handling and avoid anti-patterns such as hardcoding sensitive values or writing data to insecure locations. DevSecOps practices help ensure that security checks are embedded throughout development and deployment workflows, rather than being added as an afterthought. By automating the enforcement of storage policies and continuously scanning for misconfigurations, organizations can reduce the likelihood of accidental exposure and respond quickly when violations are detected.

Securing data at rest is not an isolated responsibility but a shared obligation across development, operations, and security teams. It requires proactive design, disciplined implementation, and continuous oversight. APIs are entrusted with some of the most valuable and sensitive assets within an organization, and the protection of stored data reflects the seriousness with which that trust is upheld. By employing strong encryption, enforcing strict access controls, minimizing data collection, and monitoring storage systems vigilantly, organizations can ensure that their APIs handle data responsibly, securely, and in alignment with both user expectations and regulatory demands.

# Secure API Gateway Architecture

An API gateway serves as the central entry point for all client requests targeting microservices or backend systems. It is responsible for routing, authentication, request transformation, monitoring, and many other cross-cutting concerns that would otherwise have to be implemented repeatedly within individual services. When architected securely, an API gateway becomes a foundational security component within an application ecosystem, acting as both a shield and a gatekeeper between external clients and internal services. The importance of securing the API gateway architecture cannot be overstated, as it typically faces the public internet, enforces access control, and handles a wide range of potentially sensitive transactions on behalf of services behind it.

The primary role of a secure API gateway is to control and mediate all external access to backend services. One of its most critical functions is enforcing strong authentication mechanisms. The gateway should require every incoming request to present valid credentials in the form of API keys, bearer tokens, or signed requests. Depending on the use case, it may also integrate with OAuth 2.0 or OpenID Connect providers to authenticate users or applications before allowing access to any protected resource. By centralizing authentication logic at the gateway level, developers reduce the attack surface and avoid redundant implementations of security logic across multiple services. A well-configured gateway only forwards authenticated and authorized requests, discarding anything that fails to meet strict access policies.

Rate limiting and throttling are also key features of a secure API gateway. These controls protect backend services from abuse, denial-of-service attacks, or accidental overuse by limiting the number of requests that a client can make in a given period. The gateway can be configured to enforce per-client limits based on IP address, user ID, or access token. These limits can be static or dynamic, adapting to usage patterns or threat intelligence data. When limits are exceeded, the gateway responds with appropriate status codes, preventing unnecessary load on internal services and preserving system stability.

The gateway also acts as a traffic inspector, applying input validation and content filtering to incoming requests. While individual services are responsible for business logic and deeper validation, the API gateway can provide a first layer of defense by rejecting malformed or malicious requests. It can inspect headers, query parameters, and body content to ensure that requests conform to expected formats and do not contain injection payloads or disallowed file types. By rejecting bad traffic early, the gateway reduces the risk of exploit attempts reaching the backend and simplifies the security model of the internal API infrastructure.

Encryption and secure communication are fundamental requirements in API gateway architecture. All external traffic must be encrypted using TLS, and the gateway should be configured to enforce HTTPS while rejecting insecure HTTP connections. Certificates must be managed carefully, using automated renewal and monitoring systems to avoid outages or trust failures. For internal traffic between the gateway and backend services, encryption should also be enforced, especially in cloud or hybrid environments where internal networks may not be inherently secure. Mutual TLS can be used to authenticate services and verify their identities before permitting communication. End-to-end encryption ensures that sensitive data remains protected from interception, even as it traverses multiple layers of infrastructure.

A secure gateway also plays a crucial role in enforcing fine-grained authorization policies. Beyond simple allow-or-deny checks, it can evaluate token scopes, user roles, or claims embedded in JWTs to determine whether the requester is permitted to perform specific actions on specific resources. These policies can be defined declaratively using policy languages or managed centrally via an access control service. Integrating authorization at the gateway level allows for consistent enforcement of rules across all APIs and services, eliminating inconsistencies and gaps in access control.

Logging and observability are essential components of a secure API gateway. Every request and response should be logged with relevant metadata, including timestamps, IP addresses, user identifiers, endpoint paths, status codes, and latency metrics. These logs must be stored securely and made available to security monitoring systems for real-time analysis and incident detection. The gateway can also emit structured metrics that feed into dashboards and alerting systems, enabling operators to detect anomalies, performance degradation, or attack patterns. Visibility at the gateway provides a complete picture of how APIs are used and where potential threats may be emerging.

Security headers are another area where the gateway can enforce best practices. The gateway should automatically attach headers like Content-Security-Policy, Strict-Transport-Security, X-Content-Type-Options, and X-Frame-Options to all responses. These headers help harden client-side security, prevent clickjacking, enforce HTTPS usage, and mitigate browser-based vulnerabilities. Centralizing this functionality within the gateway ensures that all services benefit from consistent security posture without requiring individual developers to implement these controls themselves.

In environments that adopt a zero-trust model, the API gateway becomes a vital enforcer of continuous verification. Rather than trusting any client or service by default, the gateway must verify every request based on identity, context, and policy. This includes evaluating device posture, IP reputation, and behavioral signals in addition to traditional credentials. Integrating with identity providers, threat intelligence feeds, and anomaly detection systems allows the gateway to make adaptive decisions about whether to allow, deny, or challenge a request. This dynamic evaluation improves security in scenarios where threats evolve rapidly or users operate from diverse locations and devices.

For applications that span multiple regions or cloud providers, API gateway architecture must also address geographic and multi-cloud considerations. Distributed gateways can be deployed at network edges close to users to minimize latency and improve availability. These gateways must be synchronized with consistent policies, authentication methods, and monitoring systems. Configuration drift between gateways can introduce vulnerabilities or break application functionality, so automated deployment pipelines and configuration-as-code practices are essential. When APIs are exposed globally, the gateway must enforce geofencing or jurisdictional restrictions to comply with data sovereignty laws or access control requirements based on regional risk assessments.

A secure API gateway must also be resilient. It should be capable of handling high throughput, failover, and traffic spikes without compromising security enforcement. Load balancing, horizontal scaling, and redundancy are critical to ensuring that security controls remain operational under stress. When gateways fail, they should fail securely, rejecting traffic rather than passing it through unvalidated. Built-in health checks, circuit breakers, and timeouts help maintain system integrity even during degraded states or partial outages.

The secure API gateway is not just a convenience layer but a strategic security control that defines how traffic enters, flows through, and exits the API environment. Its configuration, management, and monitoring are foundational to protecting services and data from the broad range of threats present in modern application ecosystems. By centralizing authentication, enforcing encryption, applying traffic policies, and monitoring behavior, the gateway reduces complexity and strengthens the overall security posture of the organization. It allows backend services to focus on business logic while trusting the gateway to handle the critical responsibilities of access control, validation, and protection. When designed and operated with a security-first mindset, the API gateway becomes one of the most powerful tools in securing the entire application infrastructure.

# Role of Web Application Firewalls in API Security

Web Application Firewalls, or WAFs, play a vital role in defending APIs from a wide range of web-based attacks. As APIs become more central to application ecosystems, they also become prime targets for cybercriminals. These interfaces often expose valuable backend systems and services, making them attractive to attackers looking for vulnerabilities such as injection flaws, broken authentication, misconfigurations, and data exposure. A WAF is a security component designed to detect, filter, monitor, and block malicious traffic to and from a web application or API. It acts as a gatekeeper between external clients and the API infrastructure, providing a crucial layer of defense that complements authentication, rate limiting, encryption, and other security controls already present in the system.

A WAF operates by inspecting incoming and outgoing HTTP or HTTPS traffic in real time, using a set of predefined or dynamically updated rules. These rules are designed to recognize patterns associated with common attack vectors such as SQL injection, cross-site scripting, file inclusion, command injection, and many others. For APIs, which often rely heavily on structured data formats like JSON or XML, WAFs must go beyond traditional web traffic inspection and analyze the specific characteristics of API payloads. This includes checking for malicious content embedded in request bodies, headers, or parameters that may be used to manipulate application behavior or exploit backend services.

One of the core advantages of a WAF is its ability to provide immediate protection without requiring changes to the API code. This makes it an invaluable tool for legacy systems or third-party applications where modifying the source code may not be feasible. By deploying a WAF in front of an API endpoint, security teams can enforce security policies at the network edge, reducing the likelihood that malicious requests reach the application logic. This includes not only blocking known attack patterns but also rate-limiting specific types of requests, validating protocol compliance, and preventing information disclosure through misconfigured headers or verbose error messages.

Modern WAFs often include features that adapt to evolving threats. Signature-based detection allows them to block known attack payloads using pattern recognition, while anomaly-based detection leverages behavioral models to flag traffic that deviates from the norm. For APIs, anomaly detection is particularly useful, as attacks often involve unusual sequences of operations, unexpected parameter structures, or abuse of legitimate functionality. By learning what normal API traffic looks like over time, a WAF can automatically identify and block abnormal behavior even if it does not match a known signature.

Customization is a key factor in the effectiveness of WAFs for APIs. Unlike traditional websites, APIs tend to have highly specific usage patterns, data schemas, and traffic flows. A generic rule set may generate false positives or miss subtle threats. Security teams must tailor WAF rules to match the API's expected behavior. This includes defining acceptable methods, routes, parameter formats, and data types. For example, a login endpoint should not accept GET requests with JSON payloads, and a data retrieval endpoint should not allow executable code in string fields. Enforcing such logic at the WAF layer reduces the risk of exploitation while maintaining the performance and availability of backend services.

In addition to detecting attacks, WAFs provide valuable observability into API usage. They can log all requests and responses, including metadata about the client, location, request size, and timing. These logs can be analyzed to detect suspicious patterns, investigate incidents, or refine security policies. Integration with centralized logging platforms and Security Information and Event Management (SIEM) systems enhances the ability to correlate WAF activity with broader security events across the environment. This visibility is especially important in detecting slow or low-volume attacks that may evade other forms of detection but still pose a serious threat over time.

WAFs also play a role in protecting against automated threats such as bots, scrapers, and brute-force tools. Many WAFs include built-in bot detection capabilities that identify non-human traffic based on behavioral signals, IP reputation, and header analysis. For APIs that provide access to public content, rate limits and bot protections help prevent abuse such as credential stuffing, price scraping, or denial-of-service attempts. When combined with CAPTCHA challenges, IP blacklisting, or device fingerprinting, a WAF can effectively throttle or block automated threats without disrupting legitimate users or services.

APIs that are part of microservices architectures often benefit from cloud-native WAFs that are integrated into service meshes or container orchestration platforms. These WAFs can be deployed per service or at ingress points, offering granular control and localized protection. Container-aware WAFs are particularly useful in environments where APIs are short-lived, frequently updated, or distributed across multiple clusters. They can scale with the application and apply consistent policies regardless of where the API is hosted, ensuring uniform security posture across all services.

Another emerging use case for WAFs in API environments is protection against business logic abuse. Traditional security measures focus on technical vulnerabilities, but attackers increasingly exploit flaws in the way APIs implement workflows, permissions, or data access. A WAF can be configured to enforce business logic constraints, such as preventing a user from transferring funds to themselves repeatedly, invoking a resource out of sequence, or bypassing verification steps. These protections require detailed knowledge of the API's intended use and close collaboration between developers and security teams to design effective rules that target misuse without blocking legitimate activity.

Despite their many benefits, WAFs are not a silver bullet. They must be part of a larger defense-in-depth strategy that includes secure coding practices, input validation, authentication and authorization mechanisms, encrypted communication, and regular security testing. WAFs do not replace the need for secure APIs, but they do provide an essential additional barrier that buys time, absorbs attacks, and mitigates risks before they reach the application layer. Their flexibility, real-time visibility, and integration capabilities make them a powerful tool for adapting to new threats and evolving security requirements.

The role of a Web Application Firewall in API security continues to grow as the complexity and importance of APIs increase. Whether deployed as an appliance, a cloud service, or a component of a broader security platform, a well-configured WAF can dramatically reduce the risk of exploitation, protect sensitive data, and maintain service availability in the face of constant threats. It enables organizations to enforce consistent security policies across diverse APIs, respond quickly to emerging vulnerabilities, and maintain visibility into application traffic and behavior. As APIs become the foundation of digital services, WAFs stand as one of the most reliable and dynamic defenders in the modern application security arsenal.

# Implementing API Threat Detection

In the evolving landscape of digital security, APIs have become one of the most attractive targets for attackers. As the conduits through which data flows between systems, applications, and services, APIs hold access to sensitive information and powerful operations. This makes them prime candidates for abuse, exploitation, and reconnaissance by malicious actors. Implementing effective API threat detection is critical for identifying and mitigating potential attacks before they cause damage. Threat detection goes beyond static defenses like authentication and access control; it requires ongoing observation, analysis, and response to anomalies and suspicious behavior that could indicate a security incident in progress.

The foundation of API threat detection is comprehensive visibility into all API interactions. This involves logging every request and response, including metadata such as timestamps, client IP addresses, user-agent headers, request paths, methods, payload sizes, and response statuses. These logs form the raw data that can be analyzed for patterns and anomalies. Without complete and accurate logging, detecting threats becomes a guessing game. API gateways, reverse proxies, and application firewalls are ideal points for collecting this data, as they sit at the edge of the network and can capture traffic before it reaches backend services. Additionally, instrumentation within the API code itself can provide deeper context about internal logic and application-specific behavior that external tools may miss.

Once data is collected, it must be processed and analyzed to identify indicators of compromise or misuse. Threat detection systems often rely on a combination of signature-based detection, heuristic analysis, and machine learning. Signature-based detection uses predefined patterns to recognize known attack techniques, such as SQL injection payloads or path traversal attempts. These patterns can be updated regularly as new threats emerge. Heuristic analysis evaluates the behavior of requests based on rules and policies that define what constitutes normal versus suspicious activity. For example, an unusually high number of requests to a login endpoint in a short time frame might indicate a brute-force attack. Machine learning adds a layer of adaptability, allowing the system to learn from historical data and detect subtle deviations that may not match any predefined rule.

Effective threat detection also requires correlation of events across different dimensions. A single failed login attempt may not be suspicious, but hundreds of such attempts from the same IP across different accounts can signify credential stuffing. Similarly, repeated requests to administrative endpoints from unauthenticated clients, or sudden spikes in traffic to rarely used API paths, may signal reconnaissance or probing behavior. By correlating events by time, source, endpoint, and user identity, threat detection systems can identify coordinated attacks that would otherwise appear benign when viewed in isolation. This correlation is often handled by Security Information and Event Management (SIEM) systems that ingest logs from multiple sources and apply analytics and alerting rules.

An essential aspect of API threat detection is real-time alerting. When a potentially malicious pattern is identified, the system must be capable of notifying security teams immediately. Alerts should include relevant context to allow analysts to assess severity and respond appropriately. This includes details about the source of the request, the action attempted, the affected resources, and historical data that might suggest whether the activity is part of a broader pattern. Alerts must be prioritized based on risk, with the most urgent threats triggering escalations or automated responses. Poorly tuned systems that generate excessive false positives can lead to alert fatigue, so careful configuration and tuning of detection thresholds is necessary to maintain effectiveness without overwhelming operators.

In addition to detecting threats, an API threat detection system must also support response capabilities. This includes the ability to block malicious traffic, quarantine affected accounts, revoke tokens, or ratelimit abusive clients in real time. These actions can be automated through integrations with API gateways, identity providers, or network control systems. For example, if a specific IP address is identified as the source of a denial-of-service attack, the system can dynamically update firewall rules to block further requests. If an access token is associated with suspicious behavior, the token can be revoked and the session terminated. Automation is critical in fast-moving attack scenarios where human response may be too slow to prevent damage.

Implementing threat detection also involves monitoring for misuse of legitimate functionality, known as business logic abuse. This includes actions such as repeatedly submitting refund requests, manipulating account balances, or escalating privileges through legitimate but unintended workflows. Detecting this kind of abuse requires an understanding of the API's intended behavior and the ability to define rules or baselines for acceptable usage. Application-level metrics, such as the number of password resets per user or the frequency of specific transactions, can help identify behavior that deviates from normal patterns even if it does not involve traditional exploits.

The deployment of honeypots and deception technologies can further enhance threat detection. APIs can expose decoy endpoints or credentials designed to attract attackers without granting access to real systems. Interactions with these decoys are immediately flagged as suspicious, providing early warning of probing or exploitation attempts. These techniques are particularly effective in identifying reconnaissance activity that precedes a more serious attack. By collecting intelligence on attacker behavior, security teams can strengthen defenses and update detection rules based on real-world tactics.

Threat detection is not a one-time implementation but a continuous process that must evolve with the threat landscape. Regular review of logs, alerts, and detection rules ensures that the system remains relevant and effective. As APIs change, so too must the models and assumptions used to detect threats. New endpoints, user flows, or data formats may introduce blind spots or change the behavior profile of legitimate clients. Integrating threat detection into the software development lifecycle and deploying detection capabilities alongside

API updates helps maintain alignment between the application's functionality and its security posture.

Collaboration between development, operations, and security teams is essential for successful API threat detection. Developers must understand how their APIs can be abused and provide visibility into application behavior. Operations teams must ensure that monitoring infrastructure is resilient and capable of scaling with traffic. Security teams must configure detection rules, respond to incidents, and continuously refine detection logic based on feedback and emerging threats. Threat detection is a shared responsibility that spans organizational boundaries and requires a unified strategy to be truly effective.

In the modern API ecosystem, threats are constant and increasingly sophisticated. Attackers probe for weaknesses not just in technical implementations but also in workflows, data structures, and access patterns. Implementing API threat detection provides the necessary awareness to identify these threats before they escalate into breaches. It turns passive logging into active defense, enabling organizations to anticipate, detect, and respond to attacks with speed and confidence. As APIs continue to power everything from web applications to IoT devices and financial services, robust threat detection will remain a cornerstone of secure, resilient API architecture.

# Monitoring and Logging API Activity

Monitoring and logging API activity is a critical aspect of maintaining operational visibility, ensuring security, and supporting compliance within modern digital infrastructures. APIs serve as the connective tissue of applications, linking services, clients, and data sources across increasingly distributed environments. Without proper monitoring and logging in place, organizations are essentially blind to the behavior of their systems and the actions of users. This lack of visibility can lead to undetected security breaches, prolonged outages, data loss, and an inability to respond to incidents effectively. By implementing comprehensive monitoring and logging strategies, organizations can maintain situational awareness, troubleshoot problems quickly, detect anomalies, and build a strong foundation for proactive defense and performance optimization.

Logging is the act of recording events and data associated with API activity. Every request to an API generates metadata that should be captured, including the request method, endpoint, headers, IP address, timestamp, user identity, request payload size, response status code, and processing time. These logs are essential for auditing user actions, identifying usage patterns, tracking performance issues, and correlating events across different parts of the system. Logs must be consistent, structured, and complete to be truly useful. Structured logging formats such as JSON enable easier parsing, searching, and analysis by log aggregation tools and security information and event management systems.

Effective logging requires attention to both completeness and security. It is vital to capture all relevant data without logging sensitive information that could compromise user privacy or security. Credentials, passwords, access tokens, and personally identifiable information should never be recorded in logs. Instead, logs should focus on operational data that enables tracing and troubleshooting without exposing sensitive details. Data masking and redaction techniques can be used to sanitize log entries, ensuring that logs remain useful while complying with regulations and protecting against data leakage.

In addition to request and response metadata, APIs should log internal events that provide context for the system's state. These include authentication attempts, authorization failures, rate limit violations, exceptions thrown during processing, database errors, and external service timeouts. Logging such events helps create a complete picture of what happens before, during, and after each API call. This level of detail is crucial for root cause analysis during incidents and for forensic investigations following security breaches. Logs also support the detection of abnormal patterns, such as repeated failed login attempts that might indicate a brute-force attack, or unexpected spikes in request volume that could signal a denial-of-service attempt.

Monitoring, while closely related to logging, focuses on real-time observation and analysis of system performance and behavior.

Monitoring tools collect metrics from APIs, such as request rates, error rates, latency distributions, throughput, and resource utilization. These metrics provide a continuous pulse on the health and efficiency of API services. Dashboards visualize this data in real time, allowing operators to identify performance bottlenecks, capacity issues, or failures as they happen. Monitoring also supports alerting mechanisms that notify teams when predefined thresholds are breached. For example, a sudden increase in 500-level response codes might trigger an alert to investigate backend service failures.

Combining monitoring with logging enables powerful diagnostic capabilities. When an alert indicates a performance issue, logs can be used to investigate the precise requests that led to the problem. This end-to-end visibility is especially important in microservices architectures, where requests may pass through many components before completing. Distributed tracing technologies further enhance this visibility by correlating log entries and performance metrics across services, allowing teams to reconstruct the complete journey of a request and identify which component introduced latency or errors. This unified approach accelerates incident response, reduces mean time to resolution, and improves system reliability.

API activity monitoring also plays a vital role in detecting security incidents. By continuously analyzing logs and metrics, systems can identify suspicious behavior patterns such as access from unusual geographic locations, rapid token usage, or attempts to access unauthorized resources. Security analytics platforms can process logs using correlation rules and anomaly detection algorithms to surface these threats in real time. Additionally, API access patterns can be compared against historical baselines to detect deviations that may indicate compromise. For example, a service account suddenly making requests to a previously unused endpoint might warrant investigation.

Another important aspect of monitoring and logging is supporting compliance and audit requirements. Regulations such as GDPR, HIPAA, and PCI DSS often mandate the retention of access logs and audit trails for a specified period. These logs must demonstrate who accessed which data, when, and from where. Having complete, tamper-evident logs enables organizations to prove compliance, respond to legal inquiries, and maintain accountability. Centralized logging systems with access control and integrity verification features help ensure that logs are stored securely and are not susceptible to unauthorized alteration or deletion.

The choice of tooling is critical to the success of any monitoring and logging initiative. Centralized log aggregation platforms such as the ELK stack (Elasticsearch, Logstash, Kibana), Splunk, or cloud-native solutions like AWS CloudWatch, Azure Monitor, and Google Cloud Operations Suite offer scalable infrastructure for collecting, storing, and analyzing large volumes of log data. Metrics collection tools like Prometheus, combined with visualization platforms like Grafana, provide real-time insight into system health. These tools must be integrated into the deployment pipeline and maintained alongside application code to ensure that observability remains accurate and up to date.

APIs must also expose health check endpoints that can be monitored by automated systems to confirm service availability. These endpoints should return lightweight responses indicating whether the API and its dependencies are operational. More advanced health checks can include database connectivity, cache availability, and external service status. By periodically polling these endpoints, monitoring systems can detect outages or degraded performance early and trigger automated failover or scaling actions as needed.

It is essential to implement proper log retention and lifecycle policies. Logs should be kept long enough to support debugging, auditing, and compliance needs, but not so long that they become a liability or incur unnecessary storage costs. Automated retention policies can archive or delete logs based on age, relevance, or content type. In high-security environments, logs must be encrypted at rest and in transit, and access to logs should be restricted to authorized personnel only.

Monitoring and logging are not merely operational concerns; they are core pillars of API governance, security, and performance assurance. As APIs become more integral to business operations, the ability to observe their behavior in real time and reconstruct past activity becomes indispensable. Without robust monitoring and logging, issues go undetected, threats remain hidden, and organizations lose control over their digital infrastructure. By investing in structured logging, real-time metrics, distributed tracing, and automated alerting, teams can maintain control, respond to incidents swiftly, and build systems that are both secure and resilient in the face of constant change and evolving threats.

# Versioning APIs Without Breaking Security

API versioning is a fundamental part of maintaining software over time, allowing developers to introduce changes, improvements, and new features without disrupting existing clients. However, versioning is not just a technical or structural concern; it carries significant implications for the security of the system. When APIs evolve, older versions often remain in use by clients that have not yet migrated. These legacy versions can become overlooked or poorly maintained, creating gaps in security coverage that attackers may exploit. To version APIs without breaking security, it is essential to treat each version as a fully supported and independently secured surface that must receive the same attention, controls, and monitoring as the latest release.

One of the most common approaches to API versioning involves embedding the version number in the URL path. This method is intuitive and makes it easy to route requests to the appropriate backend logic. For example, an endpoint like /v1/users is clearly distinct from /v2/users, allowing both versions to coexist. However, when older versions remain active, they must not be allowed to operate under relaxed security assumptions. Each version should undergo the same authentication and authorization checks, use the same transport-level security standards, and be subject to the same input validation and rate-limiting policies. Any deviation in these controls can create an inconsistent security posture and expose sensitive functionality to unintended misuse.

Authentication mechanisms must remain consistent across all API versions. If a new version introduces token-based authentication or a more secure OAuth flow, the older versions should be retrofitted with the same improvements, or clearly marked as deprecated with limited functionality. Allowing older versions to continue accepting less secure authentication methods, such as API keys in query strings or unencrypted credentials, creates an easy target for attackers who often probe for outdated implementations. Security teams must track which versions support which methods and ensure clients are aware of and encouraged to transition to more secure authentication models. Wherever possible, clients should be prevented from using outdated security practices, even on older versions of the API.

Authorization policies also need to be reviewed carefully during version transitions. If the access model changes, such as introducing role-based or attribute-based access control, these enhancements should not be limited to the latest version alone. Leaving older versions with weaker authorization logic undermines the overall security model. Attackers may target the version that has the least restrictive access rules to extract data or perform actions that are otherwise restricted. Each version should enforce the principle of least privilege and support fine-grained access control that reflects the current security policies of the organization.

Another critical consideration in API versioning is the evolution of data models. Changing the structure of requests and responses often introduces new fields, removes deprecated ones, or alters formats. These changes can inadvertently affect security controls if not handled with care. For example, removing a field that was previously used to verify user input might open a path for unvalidated data. Adding a new field that accepts input but failing to validate or sanitize it could create an injection vector. Whenever data models change between versions, the associated validation logic must be updated and tested rigorously to ensure that new attack surfaces are not introduced. APIs should reject unexpected fields and enforce strict schemas to prevent abuse through parameter pollution or hidden input.

Logging and monitoring must be extended across all API versions equally. It is not uncommon for organizations to focus their observability efforts on the latest version, assuming older versions are stable or low risk. This mindset is dangerous. Older versions may have known vulnerabilities or be operating with business logic that is no longer aligned with the organization's threat model. If logs from those versions are incomplete, inconsistently structured, or stored in separate systems, it becomes difficult to detect and investigate incidents that involve them. Unified logging formats, centralized monitoring, and consistent alerting thresholds ensure that all versions are visible to security teams and that anomalies can be detected no matter where they occur in the system.

Deprecation and retirement of old versions is an essential part of version management that directly impacts security. Every API version should be introduced with a clear lifecycle policy that includes a sunset date. Clients should be notified well in advance and provided with migration guides and support. Deprecating old versions without proper communication can lead to breakage and user dissatisfaction, but keeping them alive indefinitely creates long-term security debt. At the end of a version's lifecycle, access should be phased out through usage caps, rate limits, or outright disablement. When retiring a version, it is important to revoke all credentials, disable routing, and clean up any stored data associated with its usage.

Security testing must be included in every stage of the versioning process. New versions should undergo penetration testing and code review before release, but older versions should not be excluded from testing cycles. Automated scanning and fuzz testing should be performed against all active versions to detect regressions or newly discovered vulnerabilities. Regression testing is especially important because developers may assume that changes in the new version do not affect older versions, leading to missed dependencies or shared components that contain flaws. Continuous integration pipelines should include security checks for all versions being maintained, ensuring that improvements and patches are distributed evenly.

Rate limiting and throttling must also be version-aware. Different versions of the same endpoint may have different performance characteristics or handle different levels of traffic. Applying uniform rate limits may not be sufficient, especially if an older version is more susceptible to denial-of-service or resource exhaustion attacks. Each version should have configurable rate policies that reflect its usage patterns, known vulnerabilities, and performance limitations. This segmentation ensures that abuse of one version does not affect the availability or reliability of others.

Finally, documentation and education are vital components of secure versioning. API documentation should clearly indicate the security features and requirements of each version. If certain versions are missing security enhancements present in others, this must be disclosed, along with recommendations to upgrade. Clients should be provided with migration paths that emphasize not just functional improvements but also the security benefits of moving to a newer version. Encouraging developers to adopt security-conscious usage patterns and migrate away from deprecated versions contributes to a stronger overall ecosystem.

Versioning APIs without breaking security requires more than managing feature sets and compatibility. It demands a disciplined approach that treats every version as a first-class citizen in the security model. From authentication and authorization to validation, monitoring, and retirement, each step in the versioning lifecycle must be aligned with the organization's broader security objectives. Maintaining consistency, visibility, and control across versions enables teams to deliver new functionality with confidence while protecting users, data, and infrastructure from evolving threats.

# Secure Error Handling and Messaging

Error handling and messaging are often overlooked components in API design, but they play a critical role in the security and usability of an application. While developers tend to focus on ensuring that errors are caught and reported correctly, the way errors are communicated to clients can inadvertently expose sensitive information or provide attackers with insights that assist in exploitation. Secure error handling is not just about managing failures; it is about controlling the visibility of those failures and ensuring that error messages are informative for legitimate users while being opaque and unhelpful to malicious actors. The balance between clarity and concealment is at the heart of secure error messaging.

In a well-designed API, errors are inevitable. Clients will make invalid requests, authentication may fail, backend services may time out, and data may be corrupted or unavailable. Each of these situations must be handled gracefully by the API without causing system crashes or undefined behavior. More importantly, the response sent back to the client must be sanitized, consistent, and aligned with the organization's security posture. Error responses should be designed not to leak implementation details, stack traces, database query fragments, or internal configuration data that could give an attacker a clearer view of how the system works internally.

One of the most common mistakes in error messaging is providing overly verbose responses. During development, it is useful to return detailed information about an exception, including the line number, function name, or error message from a third-party library. However, in production environments, such messages become liabilities. If an attacker sends intentionally malformed input and receives an error revealing the database engine in use or the specific structure of a backend service, they gain valuable information that can guide a more targeted attack. For example, a message that states "invalid SQL syntax near 'DROP TABLE'" confirms not only the presence of a SQL database but also suggests that the input was not properly sanitized or parameterized.

Secure error handling requires that error messages be abstracted and generalized. Instead of revealing the underlying cause, messages should indicate the nature of the failure in a vague but useful manner. For example, rather than saying "username not found" or "password incorrect," a secure API should respond with a unified message like "invalid credentials." This prevents user enumeration attacks in which an attacker probes the API to determine valid usernames. Similarly, error responses for permission issues should not reveal whether the resource exists or whether the user simply lacks access. Saying "access denied" is more secure than "resource not found" if the resource does in fact exist but the requester lacks authorization.

Consistency in error formatting is also a crucial part of secure messaging. APIs should adopt a standard error response structure, such as an object containing an error code, a message, and optionally a correlation ID or timestamp. Standardization makes it easier for legitimate clients to handle errors predictably while reducing the likelihood of unintentional leaks through ad hoc error generation. The error code should map to standard HTTP status codes, such as 400 for bad requests, 401 for unauthorized, 403 for forbidden, 404 for not found, and 500 for internal server errors. Custom application-specific codes can be layered on top to provide more granular information without exposing sensitive implementation details.

When handling unexpected errors, APIs must ensure that the server continues to behave predictably. Uncaught exceptions should not crash the application or lead to inconsistent states. A global exception handler or middleware layer should catch all errors, log the full details securely on the server side, and return a sanitized error response to the client. These logs should include stack traces and diagnostic details for internal debugging, but none of that information should ever be sent back to the client. Logging and alerting systems must be in place to notify operators when unexpected errors occur, enabling timely investigation and resolution without compromising client-facing security.

Input validation plays a major role in preventing errors from occurring in the first place. Malformed inputs should be caught early in the request lifecycle, and the response should indicate what part of the input was invalid without echoing the full content of the request. For instance, if a user submits a request with an incorrectly formatted date, the API can respond with an error code and a message like "invalid date format provided" without repeating the user's input in the message. This reduces the risk of reflected input attacks and helps prevent inadvertent exposure of data that may be embedded in the request.

Another important consideration is rate limiting error responses. If an API generates a verbose error for every invalid request, it can become a useful tool for attackers to perform reconnaissance or brute-force attempts. By limiting the frequency of error messages sent to the same client or IP address, the API can discourage automated probing. Additionally, returning generic errors or introducing random delays can frustrate automated scripts that rely on consistent and predictable error responses to map out an API's behavior.

Error handling must also account for integration with external services. When a backend API depends on a third-party provider, failure responses must be carefully filtered before being returned to the client. It is not uncommon for upstream services to return detailed error messages that include information about their infrastructure, such as server names, request IDs, or even source code locations. These should never be passed through directly. Instead, the API should catch such upstream errors, log them for internal review, and return a clean error message that simply states that the operation could not be completed.

Security headers can be used in conjunction with error responses to add an additional layer of protection. Headers like Content-Type must be correctly set to prevent content sniffing, and headers such as X-Content-Type-Options and X-Frame-Options can help mitigate client-side attacks that attempt to exploit rendering behavior. Even in the case of an error, the response must adhere to the same standards and controls as successful responses to maintain a consistent and secure posture.

Education and governance are also key to achieving secure error handling. Developers must be trained to recognize the risks of verbose errors and the importance of consistent messaging. Secure coding guidelines should include error-handling practices, and code reviews must verify that exceptions are caught and handled appropriately. Automated static analysis tools can assist in identifying insecure error paths that expose sensitive details or fail to validate user input properly.

Secure error handling and messaging are not optional enhancements but essential defenses in any API ecosystem. They prevent attackers from gaining insights into system behavior, protect user privacy, and support robust and resilient application design. Every error, no matter how trivial it may seem, represents a potential opportunity for exploitation if not handled with care. By building a structured, consistent, and secure approach to error responses, APIs can maintain both usability for legitimate clients and a hardened surface against adversaries.

# API Security Testing with OWASP Tools

Ensuring the security of an API requires more than just strong design principles and best practices. It demands continuous testing, validation, and monitoring to detect vulnerabilities that could be exploited by attackers. The Open Web Application Security Project, or OWASP, provides a wealth of tools, resources, and methodologies designed to help developers and security professionals assess and improve the security posture of their APIs. OWASP's tools are widely recognized for their effectiveness in identifying common flaws, automating complex security checks, and supporting manual penetration testing efforts. These tools are grounded in the extensive research and community expertise that OWASP has developed through initiatives like the OWASP API Security Top 10, a project specifically aimed at cataloging the most prevalent and dangerous threats to APIs.

A core concept in API security testing is that every input must be treated as untrusted. OWASP tools help to validate how APIs handle untrusted input by simulating both typical usage and malicious behavior. One of the most commonly used tools in this regard is OWASP ZAP, or Zed Attack Proxy. ZAP is an open-source security scanner that allows testers to intercept API traffic, analyze requests and responses, and execute automated or manual attacks. With its proxy-based architecture, ZAP can capture all API interactions, giving testers full visibility into endpoints, parameters, authentication tokens, and data flows. It includes features such as passive scanning to identify vulnerabilities without altering traffic, and active scanning to send crafted payloads intended to exploit known weaknesses like injection flaws, broken authentication, and excessive data exposure.

Using OWASP ZAP, testers can assess whether an API is vulnerable to injection attacks by analyzing how it responds to manipulated inputs. ZAP's attack modules can insert payloads into query parameters, headers, JSON bodies, and form fields to evaluate how well the API sanitizes and validates user input. For example, by injecting SQL commands or script tags into a parameter, ZAP can test whether the API backend is susceptible to SQL injection or cross-site scripting. These tests reveal whether input is being improperly concatenated into queries or reflected back to the client without proper encoding. In APIs that accept complex input structures, such as deeply nested JSON, ZAP can analyze how different nesting levels and payload sizes affect the application's behavior, potentially uncovering flaws related to deserialization or buffer overflow.

OWASP Amass is another powerful tool in the API security tester's arsenal. While ZAP focuses on the behavior of the API once it is known, Amass supports reconnaissance and asset discovery. It helps testers identify subdomains, APIs exposed through DNS entries, and associated infrastructure components. This is particularly useful in large organizations where shadow APIs may exist outside of central control or documentation. Discovering these hidden interfaces is a crucial step in developing a complete understanding of the attack surface. Attackers often exploit forgotten or deprecated endpoints that still process data or accept input. By scanning DNS records, WHOIS information, and certificate transparency logs, Amass helps uncover these assets so they can be secured or decommissioned.

The OWASP API Security Top 10 serves as a reference framework for what to test when using OWASP tools. Each item on the list represents a critical category of risk, such as broken object-level authorization, security misconfigurations, or lack of rate limiting. For example, OWASP ZAP can be configured to test for excessive data exposure by examining API responses for verbose error messages or unnecessary fields in response objects. By intercepting traffic, ZAP can reveal whether internal implementation details, such as database IDs or debug information, are being inadvertently exposed. This kind of exposure can aid attackers in crafting more targeted attacks or manipulating business logic.

Broken authentication is another top threat category that OWASP tools can help detect. By replaying tokens, tampering with session cookies, or attempting brute-force attacks against login endpoints, ZAP can evaluate the robustness of an API's authentication mechanisms. Testers can analyze whether tokens expire properly, whether sessions can be hijacked through predictable identifiers, or whether multi-factor authentication is enforced. OWASP's tools can also help assess how well the API resists credential stuffing and other automated attacks by analyzing rate limits, CAPTCHA enforcement, and anomaly detection thresholds.

Rate limiting and denial-of-service vulnerabilities are also important to test. OWASP tools can be used to simulate high-volume traffic to see how the API responds under stress. By sending a rapid series of requests to a single endpoint, testers can evaluate whether rate limiting policies are in place and whether error messages reveal anything useful to attackers. If the API returns detailed timing information or stack traces during heavy load, these could be used as reconnaissance tools. ZAP can be extended with scripts to create custom attack payloads or flooding scenarios, allowing for targeted testing of specific rate limits or quotas.

In addition to dynamic testing, OWASP also supports static and configuration analysis. Tools like OWASP Dependency-Check can identify known vulnerabilities in the third-party libraries used by the API. This is crucial in modern applications that rely heavily on open-source components. Vulnerabilities in libraries such as web frameworks, authentication modules, or JSON parsers can introduce systemic risks that are difficult to detect through dynamic testing alone. By analyzing project dependencies against vulnerability databases like the National Vulnerability Database (NVD), Dependency-Check helps teams identify and remediate risky components before they are exploited in production.

Manual testing is another area where OWASP tools shine. ZAP, for instance, includes a robust interface for manual exploration, allowing testers to craft custom requests, modify headers, inject payloads, and observe the responses in real time. This supports deeper analysis of complex or stateful APIs that may not be easily handled by automated scanners. For APIs that use authentication protocols like OAuth 2.0 or OpenID Connect, ZAP can capture and replay the token exchange process, enabling testers to analyze how tokens are validated and whether refresh or revocation logic is functioning correctly.

Comprehensive API security testing using OWASP tools also involves integration with development workflows. ZAP and other tools can be embedded into CI/CD pipelines to provide automated scans during build and deployment stages. This allows organizations to catch regressions early, enforce security baselines, and ensure that new code does not introduce known vulnerabilities. Automated reports from OWASP tools can be reviewed by security teams or even trigger gates that prevent insecure code from being promoted to production. This proactive approach transforms security testing from a periodic, manual process into a continuous and integrated part of the software lifecycle.

OWASP tools provide a practical, open-source foundation for identifying and mitigating security risks in APIs. By combining dynamic analysis, static code evaluation, asset discovery, and manual testing capabilities, these tools enable a thorough assessment of an API's resilience against real-world attacks. Their use empowers developers and security professionals to find weaknesses early, understand the implications of their architecture, and continuously improve their API security posture in an ever-changing threat landscape.

# Protecting APIs from Denial-of-Service Attacks

Denial-of-Service attacks are among the most disruptive threats to any online service, and APIs are particularly vulnerable due to their programmability, accessibility, and role in connecting critical services. A Denial-of-Service, or DoS, attack seeks to overwhelm a service with an excessive volume of requests or resource-consuming operations, rendering it inaccessible to legitimate users. When such attacks are distributed across multiple systems, they become Distributed Denial-of-Service (DDoS) attacks, which are harder to mitigate and far more powerful in their impact. APIs, as the backend for modern applications, mobile services, IoT devices, and integrations, must be designed and protected with DoS resistance in mind from the ground up to ensure service continuity, data integrity, and resilience under pressure.

One of the primary challenges in defending APIs from DoS attacks is distinguishing between legitimate traffic and malicious traffic. Unlike traditional websites, APIs are built to support automation and programmatic access. This means a high volume of requests is not necessarily a sign of abuse. APIs might receive large bursts of traffic from mobile apps syncing data, cron jobs executing workflows, or business partners pulling reports. DoS protection must, therefore, be intelligently applied to avoid blocking legitimate clients while detecting abnormal behaviors that suggest an attack is underway. This requires visibility into request patterns, baseline behaviors, and the context in which those requests occur.

Rate limiting is one of the most effective and foundational defenses against DoS attacks. By capping the number of requests a client can make over a specific period, APIs can prevent any one user or system from monopolizing resources. Rate limits can be defined per IP address, per user token, per client application, or even per endpoint depending on the API's structure. For example, a login endpoint might have stricter rate limits than a public product catalog. Properly configured rate limits prevent brute-force attempts, protect sensitive endpoints from abuse, and reduce the likelihood of resource exhaustion. Implementing exponential backoff and cooldown periods for repeat violations further discourages aggressive behavior.

However, not all DoS attacks come from a single source. Distributed Denial-of-Service attacks involve hundreds or thousands of devices, often compromised as part of a botnet, sending requests simultaneously. To defend against these, APIs need more sophisticated measures. Traffic from known bad IP ranges can be blocked outright using threat intelligence feeds. Geo-blocking can be applied to restrict access from regions that have no legitimate users. Additionally, CAPTCHA or JavaScript challenge mechanisms, though more commonly used on websites, can be adapted for APIs in the form of token challenges or puzzle-based request throttling for suspicious traffic. These techniques raise the cost of an attack by requiring additional computation or interaction from the client.

A secure API gateway plays a critical role in managing and mitigating DoS threats. Gateways can inspect requests in real time and apply layered security controls before passing traffic to backend services. This includes rate limiting, IP filtering, and protocol validation to block malformed or oversized requests. Some API gateways also offer automatic scaling or circuit breaker functionality that protects backend services by rejecting requests once a predefined threshold of errors, latency, or load has been reached. This protects internal infrastructure from cascading failures when under stress. Circuit breakers can also be used to isolate specific endpoints or client tokens exhibiting unusual behavior without affecting the availability of the entire API.

Load balancing is another essential part of DoS resilience. By distributing incoming requests across multiple servers, load balancers prevent any single machine from being overwhelmed. In a cloud-native architecture, auto-scaling capabilities can spin up additional instances to handle temporary surges in demand. However, scaling alone is not a complete solution. It can be expensive, and without proper rate limiting and filtering, attackers can still exhaust system limits or inflate costs. Thus, scaling must be combined with other preventative measures to ensure that only legitimate demand results in increased resource allocation.

Application-level protections are equally important. APIs must be written to handle overload conditions gracefully. This includes rejecting requests when system health is degraded, queuing requests when backend capacity is temporarily exceeded, and avoiding long-running operations that tie up server threads or memory. Lightweight responses such as HTTP 429 Too Many Requests or 503 Service Unavailable, returned with appropriate headers, inform clients that service is temporarily constrained and can help automate retries using backoff strategies. Monitoring systems should track these responses and alert operators when thresholds are crossed, enabling rapid incident response and capacity planning.

Monitoring and logging are vital in the defense against DoS attacks. Real-time dashboards that track request rates, error codes, latency, and system health provide visibility into potential attacks as they unfold. Logs must be structured and centralized to allow rapid correlation of events across nodes. Alerts can be configured to trigger when sudden traffic spikes occur, when unusual patterns are detected on specific endpoints, or when known indicators of compromise appear in request headers or payloads. Observability tools also assist in forensic analysis after an attack, helping teams understand the source, scope, and impact, and refine protections accordingly.

Web Application Firewalls are another layer of protection. A WAF sits in front of an API and filters traffic based on rules and behavioral analysis. WAFs can block common attack patterns such as HTTP floods, protocol anomalies, and known bot signatures. They can also analyze the intent of incoming requests using anomaly detection models and apply dynamic rules to suppress malicious traffic. When integrated with an API management platform, a WAF enhances visibility and control, allowing teams to enforce policies across environments and adapt quickly to emerging threats.

Authentication and authorization controls, while primarily aimed at preventing unauthorized access, also help limit DoS risks by reducing the number of unauthenticated endpoints and ensuring that sensitive operations are protected. Public APIs should be carefully scoped and monitored, while internal and private APIs must enforce strict authentication with token expiration and scope-limiting mechanisms. Anonymous or free-tier clients should be subject to lower rate limits and more rigorous validation, while trusted clients may be given greater access but with more frequent behavior monitoring.

Ultimately, defending against Denial-of-Service attacks requires a layered strategy that combines preventive measures, real-time detection, and rapid response capabilities. No single tool or setting is sufficient. Instead, APIs must be designed and operated with resilience in mind, ensuring that the system remains available and secure even under duress. As the number of APIs in production environments continues to grow, and as attackers become more sophisticated in targeting them, organizations must invest in comprehensive DoS protection strategies that evolve alongside their infrastructure. The goal is not only to survive an attack but to maintain trust, performance, and operational stability in the face of ongoing threats.

# API Access Control Models: RBAC, ABAC, and PBAC

Access control is a cornerstone of API security, ensuring that only authorized users or systems can access specific resources or perform designated actions. Without effective access control, an API becomes vulnerable to unauthorized data access, privilege escalation, and abuse of functionality. As APIs continue to evolve in complexity and scale, organizations must adopt flexible and granular access control models that can adapt to diverse user needs, dynamic contexts, and regulatory requirements. Among the most widely used models in the context of API security are Role-Based Access Control (RBAC), Attribute-Based

Access Control (ABAC), and Policy-Based Access Control (PBAC). Each model offers distinct advantages and is suited to different environments, use cases, and levels of complexity.

Role-Based Access Control is one of the most established and widely implemented models for managing access to APIs. In RBAC, permissions are assigned to roles rather than directly to users. Users are then assigned one or more roles based on their responsibilities or functions within the organization. For example, a user assigned the role of administrator may have access to create, update, and delete resources, while a user with the viewer role may only have read access. This abstraction simplifies the management of permissions, especially in large organizations, by reducing the need to assign permissions individually. In API environments, RBAC is often enforced by associating each API endpoint or action with a specific role or set of roles. When a request is received, the system checks the roles associated with the authenticated user and determines whether the requested operation is permitted.

The simplicity of RBAC makes it highly effective in environments with clearly defined user roles and stable access requirements. It supports separation of duties and limits access to the minimum necessary level, aligning with the principle of least privilege. However, RBAC has limitations in scenarios where access decisions must take into account contextual information beyond the user's role. For instance, it cannot easily enforce rules like allowing a manager to view only the records of employees in their department or restricting access based on the time of day or location of the request. As systems become more dynamic and access control requirements more nuanced, RBAC may struggle to keep up without an explosion in the number of roles and role combinations.

Attribute-Based Access Control offers a more flexible and granular alternative to RBAC. ABAC makes access decisions based on attributes associated with the user, the resource, the action, and the environment. Attributes can include user properties like department, clearance level, or job title; resource properties such as classification, owner, or sensitivity; and environmental properties like IP address, time, or device type. In ABAC, policies are written as logical rules that evaluate these attributes to determine whether access should be granted. For example, a policy might state that a user can access a document if they belong to the same department as the document owner and the request occurs during business hours.

ABAC excels in environments where access rules are complex and dynamic. It allows for more adaptive and precise control by considering multiple dimensions of the access context. APIs that serve diverse clients with varying needs—such as enterprise platforms, healthcare systems, or government applications—benefit from the fine-grained policies enabled by ABAC. The challenge with ABAC lies in its complexity. Defining, managing, and maintaining attribute-based policies requires careful planning, consistent attribute definitions, and governance processes to ensure policies are not overly permissive or contradictory. ABAC systems also rely on the integrity and accuracy of attribute data, which must be kept current and secure to maintain effective access control.

Policy-Based Access Control builds upon the principles of ABAC but adds a layer of abstraction and standardization by defining access control rules as centralized policies. PBAC allows organizations to externalize authorization logic from application code, placing it into a policy engine that evaluates requests against a defined set of rules. These rules can incorporate both RBAC-style roles and ABAC-style attributes, offering a hybrid approach that supports a wide range of access scenarios. PBAC is particularly valuable in environments where access decisions must be consistent across multiple systems and services, or where regulatory compliance requires centralized oversight and auditability.

With PBAC, policies are typically written in a domain-specific language or standard such as the eXtensible Access Control Markup Language (XACML) or Rego, the policy language used by the Open Policy Agent (OPA). The policy engine evaluates incoming API requests by matching the request context against defined policies, which specify who can access what under which conditions. This model promotes reusability, scalability, and central governance, allowing security teams to update access control logic without modifying application code. For APIs, PBAC enables consistent enforcement across microservices, cloud applications, and third-party integrations, reducing the risk of inconsistent or outdated access logic.

The implementation of any access control model in an API requires careful consideration of identity management, token design, and request context propagation. Identity providers and authentication systems must supply reliable claims about the user or system making the request. These claims, often embedded in tokens such as JSON Web Tokens (JWT), carry the necessary information for access decisions, including roles, attributes, and scopes. API gateways and middleware must be configured to extract and validate this information, passing it along to backend services or policy engines as needed. Proper handling of identity claims is essential to prevent impersonation, token forgery, or misuse of elevated privileges.

Auditing and monitoring access decisions is a crucial part of securing access control implementations. APIs must log each access request along with the outcome of the access control evaluation, including the policy or rule that led to the decision. These logs support compliance reporting, forensic investigations, and policy refinement. In complex systems, visibility into why a request was allowed or denied is key to diagnosing access issues and ensuring that policies function as intended. Tools that provide policy analysis, testing, and visualization help reduce the risk of misconfiguration and make access control more transparent and manageable.

Choosing the right access control model depends on the nature of the application, the sensitivity of the data, the diversity of the user base, and the complexity of the access rules. RBAC is well suited for systems with well-defined roles and straightforward permissions. ABAC is ideal for environments requiring dynamic, context-aware decisions. PBAC offers centralized, scalable control for distributed and regulated environments. In practice, many organizations adopt a hybrid approach, combining elements of all three models to meet their needs. Regardless of the model, effective access control is essential to safeguarding APIs against unauthorized access, data leakage, and abuse, forming a core pillar of any comprehensive API security strategy.

# Protecting APIs in Microservices Architectures

The adoption of microservices architectures has transformed the way modern applications are built, deployed, and scaled. In a microservices model, applications are broken into small, independently deployable services that communicate primarily through APIs. This architectural style offers significant advantages in terms of agility, scalability, and fault isolation, but it also introduces a broad and complex attack surface. Unlike monolithic applications with a single API gateway or perimeter, microservices environments often involve hundreds or thousands of APIs that communicate over internal networks. Securing these APIs requires a new mindset and a layered approach to ensure confidentiality, integrity, and availability across distributed systems.

At the heart of microservices is the principle of decentralized development. Each service is typically owned by an independent team, often developed in different languages, using different frameworks, and deployed on distinct runtimes. This decentralization makes consistency in security practices difficult to maintain. Without a standardized approach, it becomes easy for services to drift apart in terms of access control mechanisms, logging strategies, data validation rules, and encryption configurations. To counter this, organizations must enforce security policies through shared infrastructure components such as API gateways, service meshes, and centralized authentication services that provide guardrails without limiting team autonomy.

Authentication in a microservices environment cannot rely solely on traditional session-based mechanisms. Since services are stateless and scale dynamically, session management becomes impractical. Token-based authentication, particularly using JSON Web Tokens, is the preferred method. Clients authenticate once, receive a signed token, and present this token with each request. Downstream services verify the token's signature and claims without needing to contact a central authentication server, allowing for high scalability and low latency. However, tokens must be carefully designed to include only necessary claims, avoid excessive lifetimes, and use strong cryptographic signing algorithms to prevent forgery or tampering.

Once a request is authenticated at the edge, the identity and authorization context must be propagated securely throughout the call chain. This is often referred to as service-to-service authentication or internal request trust. It is not sufficient to assume that a request arriving from within the internal network is safe. Each service must authenticate and authorize every incoming request based on its identity, not merely its origin. Mutual TLS provides a strong foundation for this by ensuring that both the client and the server can prove their identities using certificates. When combined with access control policies that enforce role or attribute-based rules, mutual TLS establishes trust in both directions and prevents unauthorized lateral movement within the service mesh.

A major concern in microservices architectures is the exposure of internal APIs. While some APIs are meant to be consumed by external clients, others are designed solely for internal use. Without proper segmentation, internal APIs may become exposed to the public or even to other services that should not access them. Network policies, firewall rules, and service mesh configurations should enforce strict segmentation and zero trust principles, ensuring that only explicitly authorized services can communicate. This minimizes the risk of compromise spreading across service boundaries and provides better control over data flows.

Data protection is another key element. Since microservices often process sensitive data across multiple components, encryption of data both in transit and at rest is non-negotiable. All API communication, including internal service calls, must be encrypted using TLS. Furthermore, sensitive data handled by one service must not be exposed to others unless explicitly required. This principle of least privilege extends to data access, meaning that services should only request and receive the minimum data necessary to perform their function. Token scopes and data masking techniques help enforce this by limiting the visibility of claims or payload content based on service roles.

Monitoring and observability are critical for maintaining security in a distributed system. Unlike monoliths where logs and metrics are centralized by design, microservices can generate vast amounts of telemetry across multiple hosts and runtimes. To detect potential threats and performance issues, organizations must implement centralized logging and monitoring solutions that aggregate logs, metrics, and traces from all services. Tools such as distributed tracing allow security teams to follow a request as it traverses various services, helping to identify anomalies, unauthorized access attempts, or failures in the call chain. Logs must include request identifiers, timestamps, user context, and authorization outcomes to support effective forensic analysis.

Rate limiting and abuse protection must also be reimagined in a microservices world. Attackers may target one service to exhaust resources or trigger cascading failures. Services should implement rate limits at multiple levels, including client-facing endpoints, internal APIs, and backend operations. A common pattern is to apply global rate limits at the API gateway and fine-grained limits within individual services. This layered approach helps contain abusive behavior while preserving availability. Services that rely on shared resources such as databases or caches must guard against resource starvation by implementing circuit breakers, bulkheads, and retry budgets.

The deployment and lifecycle management of microservices introduces additional security concerns. With frequent updates and ephemeral instances, there is a higher chance of configuration errors, stale credentials, or unpatched vulnerabilities. DevSecOps practices must be integrated into the CI/CD pipeline to ensure that each service is scanned, tested, and validated before deployment. Security controls such as static code analysis, dependency vulnerability scanning, and configuration validation should be automated and enforced at build time. Secrets management must also be handled centrally, with credentials injected at runtime through secure vaults or environment-specific secret providers rather than hardcoded or stored in source code.

Finally, incident response in a microservices environment must be adapted to deal with distributed complexity. When a security event occurs, responders need tools to quickly identify which service is affected, what data may have been exposed, and how the incident propagated. Well-documented service inventories, dependency graphs, and service-level objectives are essential for narrowing the blast radius and coordinating remediation. Each service team should participate in regular security drills and post-incident reviews to improve resilience and refine processes.

Securing APIs in microservices architectures is a multifaceted challenge that requires coordination across teams, consistent tooling, and deep visibility into inter-service communication. As the number of services grows, so too does the complexity of securing them. Through identity propagation, zero trust principles, encryption, observability, and automated governance, organizations can build a robust framework for protecting APIs in even the most dynamic and large-scale microservices deployments. The focus must always remain on minimizing trust assumptions, controlling data flows, and ensuring that every interaction—whether internal or external—is explicitly authorized and transparently monitored.

# Zero Trust Principles for API Security

The concept of zero trust has emerged as a transformative security paradigm in response to the growing complexity of digital environments, the dissolution of traditional perimeters, and the increasing sophistication of cyber threats. At its core, zero trust is based on the principle of never automatically trusting any request, device, or user, regardless of their location in the network. In the context of APIs, which serve as gateways to data and services across distributed systems, zero trust principles are particularly crucial. APIs often span cloud and on-premises environments, mobile and web applications, and internal microservices, making them prime targets for exploitation. Zero trust for APIs means verifying every interaction, minimizing implicit trust, and enforcing strict controls at every stage of communication.

Traditional perimeter-based security models assume that anything inside the network can be trusted. This assumption fails in modern environments where APIs are consumed by external partners, cloud workloads, and services deployed across multiple platforms. Zero trust replaces this outdated model with a new approach in which every request to an API is treated as potentially malicious until it is explicitly authenticated, authorized, and evaluated against dynamic security policies. This shift requires fundamental changes to how APIs are designed, deployed, and governed, but it also enables greater resilience, adaptability, and precision in protecting critical digital assets.

Authentication is the first pillar of zero trust applied to APIs. Every API request must come with a valid, verifiable identity. This means enforcing strong authentication mechanisms that support both human users and machine identities. For human users, this involves multi-factor authentication and identity federation, while for machines and applications, secure issuance and validation of credentials such as certificates, tokens, and keys are essential. JSON Web Tokens, OAuth 2.0 access tokens, and mTLS certificates must be validated not only for authenticity but also for expiration, issuer, audience, and scope. The identity of the caller must be established with certainty before the request is allowed to proceed.

However, zero trust does not stop at authentication. Authorization must follow immediately, ensuring that the authenticated entity is allowed to access the requested resource and perform the intended action. Authorization decisions must be contextual and granular. They should consider the sensitivity of the resource, the action being taken, the current risk level, and attributes of the user or service making the request. This requires APIs to adopt fine-grained access control models, such as attribute-based or policy-based authorization, and to externalize authorization logic to ensure consistency across services. Policies must be centrally managed and dynamically enforced to reflect the changing conditions of the system, including the presence of new threats or emerging vulnerabilities.

Least privilege is a foundational tenet of zero trust that must be strictly applied to API design and usage. Every API client should be granted the minimum level of access necessary to perform its function. This applies to users, services, third-party applications, and automated scripts. Overly permissive API tokens or access keys are a common source of data exposure and lateral movement during breaches. APIs should support token scopes, role restrictions, and time-limited credentials that automatically expire. Access should be routinely reviewed and revoked when no longer needed. By limiting the potential damage that any one token or user can cause, the system becomes inherently more secure and resilient to compromise.

Visibility and inspection of API traffic are also essential under a zero trust model. Every request, regardless of its origin or apparent legitimacy, should be logged, monitored, and analyzed. This level of observability allows organizations to detect unusual patterns, identify compromised accounts, and respond to emerging threats. Monitoring should include metadata such as IP addresses, geolocation, device types, and behavioral patterns, as well as content inspection where appropriate. Anomalous behavior, such as a sudden increase in request volume or unexpected access to sensitive endpoints, must trigger alerts or automated responses. Observability tools must be tightly integrated with security information and event management systems to provide real-time intelligence and support forensic investigations.

Encryption of data in transit is non-negotiable in a zero trust API ecosystem. All API traffic must be encrypted using strong TLS protocols to protect against eavesdropping, tampering, and man-in-the-middle attacks. Even internal service-to-service communication within the same network zone must be encrypted. Zero trust assumes that the network is hostile, even when it is owned and operated by the same organization. Therefore, no communication path is exempt from encryption. In addition to encryption, APIs should verify the integrity of messages using cryptographic signatures or secure hashing to ensure that data has not been altered in transit.

Device and environmental context are increasingly relevant in zero trust API enforcement. A request's legitimacy depends not only on the identity of the requester but also on the trustworthiness of the device being used and the context in which the request is made. For example, requests originating from unmanaged devices or from geographic regions known for malicious activity may require additional verification or may be blocked altogether. Risk-adaptive access control allows systems to increase or decrease the level of scrutiny based on current conditions, enabling more nuanced security responses without compromising usability. Integrating device posture checks and threat intelligence feeds into API access decisions strengthens the system's ability to dynamically respond to risk.

Another principle of zero trust is the segmentation of resources and isolation of workloads. APIs must be grouped and protected based on their sensitivity, exposure, and usage patterns. Internal APIs should not be exposed externally without explicit review and protective controls. Each API should have its own authentication, rate limiting, and logging policies. Services must not implicitly trust one another just because they reside in the same network or cluster. Service meshes and modern API gateways can enforce these boundaries, applying identity verification, encryption, and policy checks to every call, regardless of source. Microsegmentation reduces the blast radius of any security incident and ensures that a compromise in one service does not easily lead to a breach of others.

Automation is a critical enabler of zero trust at scale. Manually managing access policies, identity verification, and threat response is unsustainable in environments with hundreds of APIs and thousands of clients. Automated systems must issue, rotate, and revoke credentials, evaluate policies, and respond to threats in real time. DevSecOps practices help integrate zero trust principles into the development lifecycle, ensuring that APIs are secure from the moment they are designed. Security-as-code frameworks enable consistent enforcement across environments and reduce the chances of human error or misconfiguration. Automated testing of authentication and authorization flows ensures that zero trust assumptions hold true even as the system evolves.

Zero trust for APIs is not a product or a setting but a mindset and a discipline. It requires continuous validation, strict control, and relentless skepticism toward every access attempt. In a world where perimeters have vanished, and threats are persistent and adaptive, the only sustainable way to protect APIs is to build systems that trust nothing and verify everything. This model not only enhances security but also supports scalability, agility, and resilience, enabling organizations to move faster without compromising their defenses. By embedding zero trust principles into every layer of the API ecosystem, organizations can ensure that access to data and services is always governed by strict controls, real-time context, and unbreakable trust boundaries.

# Container Security in API Deployments

Containers have revolutionized the way APIs are developed, deployed, and scaled. By encapsulating an application and its dependencies into a lightweight, portable package, containers offer unmatched flexibility and efficiency for running API services across diverse environments. Whether deployed in development clusters, staging environments, or production-grade orchestration systems like Kubernetes, containers allow APIs to scale rapidly, adapt to dynamic workloads, and maintain consistency across deployment stages. However, this agility introduces new challenges and risks, particularly around security. Ensuring container security in API deployments requires a thorough understanding of the container lifecycle, the associated infrastructure, and the attack surfaces that emerge from this model.

One of the most critical aspects of container security begins at the image level. Container images are the foundation from which all containers are instantiated. If the image is compromised, outdated, or improperly configured, every container that runs from it inherits those vulnerabilities. In the context of API deployments, where each image may serve requests, handle sensitive data, or interface with external systems, image integrity becomes paramount. Developers must use minimal, trusted base images and avoid including unnecessary packages or binaries that expand the attack surface. Each image should be scanned for known vulnerabilities using automated tools integrated into the CI/CD pipeline. These tools reference vulnerability databases and provide real-time feedback on outdated libraries, misconfigurations, and exploitable dependencies before the image is ever deployed.

Beyond static analysis of images, runtime security is essential to maintain a secure API deployment. Once a container is running, it must be monitored for anomalous behavior such as unexpected network connections, privilege escalations, or unauthorized file access. API containers should be configured with the principle of least privilege in mind, ensuring that each process runs with the minimum necessary permissions. Containers should not run as the root user unless absolutely necessary. Capabilities like writing to the host filesystem, executing arbitrary shell commands, or accessing sensitive host resources should be explicitly disabled. Security contexts in orchestration platforms must be configured to prevent containers from escaping their sandbox or interfering with other containers.

Another major concern is the use of secrets within containers. APIs often require credentials to connect to databases, external services, or authentication providers. Hardcoding secrets into container images or passing them as environment variables at runtime poses a serious risk. If the image is leaked or the container is compromised, attackers can extract these secrets and move laterally through the environment. Secure secret management tools such as HashiCorp Vault, AWS Secrets Manager, or Kubernetes secrets should be used to store and inject credentials securely at runtime. These tools offer encryption, access control, auditing, and automatic rotation, all of which reduce the risk of secret exposure and misuse.

Network segmentation is another layer of defense in containerized API deployments. In traditional architectures, APIs might be deployed behind a central gateway or firewall, but in a containerized environment, services are distributed across nodes and communicate internally through dynamic network interfaces. This makes it essential to enforce network policies that restrict which containers can communicate with each other. APIs should not accept traffic from unauthorized sources, and sensitive services should be accessible only through tightly controlled ingress points. Service meshes, such as Istio or Linkerd, enhance network security by providing mutual TLS encryption for all service-to-service communication, enforcing policy-based routing, and enabling fine-grained access controls that limit traffic between workloads.

Logging and monitoring are indispensable for detecting security incidents and maintaining situational awareness. Each container must emit logs that capture API request metadata, error codes, authentication events, and system-level operations. These logs must be aggregated and stored securely, often using centralized logging solutions that support correlation, indexing, and alerting. Metrics and telemetry should be collected using monitoring tools that can track the health, performance, and behavior of containers in real time. Security teams must define alerting thresholds that trigger investigations into unusual patterns, such as sudden spikes in traffic, repeated failed login attempts, or changes in API behavior that deviate from historical baselines.

Supply chain security is another key dimension of containerized API deployments. APIs are rarely built from scratch; they depend on a wide variety of third-party libraries, frameworks, and tools. These dependencies are often pulled automatically into container images during the build process. If a malicious or compromised dependency is included, it can introduce backdoors, inject malicious logic, or exfiltrate data silently. To prevent this, organizations must use software composition analysis tools that audit all dependencies, track licenses, and monitor for known vulnerabilities. Signing container images and verifying signatures at runtime provides assurance that the image has not been tampered with. This practice, combined with maintaining an internal registry of vetted images, helps reduce the risk of supply chain compromise.

Orchestration platforms such as Kubernetes introduce their own layer of complexity and risk. While these platforms offer powerful tools for scaling and managing API workloads, they also require careful configuration to avoid security pitfalls. Misconfigured access controls can allow unauthorized users to deploy or modify containers. Unrestricted APIs can expose control planes to attack. Kubernetes role-based access control must be tightly configured to limit who can deploy, modify, or access API workloads. Admission controllers can be used to enforce security policies at deployment time, such as rejecting containers that run as root or do not use a certified base image. Keeping the orchestration platform itself patched and up to date is equally critical, as vulnerabilities in the cluster can lead to complete environment compromise.

Isolation between environments is vital in containerized API deployments. Development, testing, staging, and production environments must be separated by strict boundaries, preventing test data or insecure configurations from bleeding into production. Infrastructure as code tools must define these boundaries explicitly, and automated deployments must ensure that policies, secrets, and access rights are correctly scoped to the environment. Containers in one namespace or cluster should never have access to resources in another unless explicitly permitted, and such permissions must be logged and regularly reviewed.

Security education and governance are the final, yet ongoing, requirements for successful containerized API deployments. Development and operations teams must understand the security implications of their decisions, from how containers are built to how they are monitored. Shared responsibility models must be clearly defined, ensuring that every team knows their role in maintaining security. Regular audits, vulnerability scans, and compliance checks must be embedded in workflows to maintain continuous assurance.

Container security in API deployments is not an isolated task but a continuous effort that touches every stage of the application lifecycle. From how images are built and signed to how containers are executed, monitored, and destroyed, every step introduces potential vulnerabilities that must be proactively addressed. With the right combination of tooling, policies, and cultural commitment to security, organizations can deploy APIs in containers with confidence, knowing that their workloads are protected against the ever-evolving threat landscape.

# Cloud-Native API Security Practices

The shift toward cloud-native architecture has fundamentally changed how APIs are developed, deployed, and secured. In a cloud-native ecosystem, APIs are not just interfaces for data exchange but are integral components of highly dynamic, distributed, and scalable systems. These systems leverage containers, microservices, orchestration platforms, and managed services provided by public cloud providers. With this transformation comes a new set of security requirements that must account for ephemeral workloads, elastic scaling, multi-tenancy, and complex inter-service communication. Traditional security models based on static infrastructure and perimeter defenses are insufficient. Instead, cloud-native API security practices focus on automation, declarative policy enforcement, observability, and identity-centric controls that align with the principles of cloud-native computing.

A key practice in securing cloud-native APIs is the implementation of identity and access management at every layer of interaction. Unlike traditional environments where a single firewall might guard access to an application, cloud-native APIs must be protected at multiple ingress points across regions and zones. Authentication must be token-based, stateless, and verifiable across distributed systems. This is typically achieved using OAuth 2.0, OpenID Connect, and JSON Web Tokens, which allow secure identity propagation across services. Cloud providers offer native identity services such as AWS IAM, Azure Active Directory, and Google Cloud IAM, which can be integrated with API gateways to authenticate both users and services. These identities are further enriched with roles and policies that define precise permissions, ensuring that each API call is authorized based on the principle of least privilege.

API gateways serve as critical enforcement points for cloud-native security policies. Deployed as managed services or self-hosted components, gateways provide centralized control over authentication, rate limiting, input validation, and request routing. In a cloud-native environment, the gateway also acts as the boundary between public and private traffic, shielding internal services from direct exposure. Security configurations at the gateway level include TLS termination, header sanitization, request size limits, and content inspection to prevent common web attacks such as injection, cross-site scripting, and data leakage. Advanced gateways also support API versioning and transformation rules that help maintain backward compatibility without sacrificing security.

Network security in cloud-native environments depends heavily on microsegmentation and policy-based routing. The ephemeral nature of containers and serverless functions means that network addresses cannot be used as reliable identifiers for access control. Instead, service identities and metadata are used to determine communication permissions. Service meshes like Istio and Linkerd provide fine-grained control over service-to-service traffic using mutual TLS, certificate rotation, and dynamic authorization policies. These meshes operate transparently at the network layer, enforcing encryption and identity verification without requiring code changes. Cloud-native firewalls and network policies in Kubernetes further restrict egress and ingress traffic based on labels, namespaces, and service accounts, offering defense-in-depth for API endpoints.

Observability is another cornerstone of cloud-native API security. APIs in distributed systems generate vast amounts of telemetry data, including logs, metrics, and traces. This data must be collected, aggregated, and analyzed in real time to detect anomalies, track performance, and respond to incidents. Cloud-native monitoring platforms such as Prometheus, Grafana, CloudWatch, and Azure Monitor provide the tooling to visualize API activity and set alerting thresholds. Centralized logging systems like Elasticsearch or Fluentd capture structured logs from all services, enabling threat detection, audit trails, and forensic analysis. The combination of observability and automation allows for the deployment of behavioral detection models that can identify unusual patterns, such as a spike in failed authentication attempts or repeated access to sensitive endpoints.

Infrastructure as code is another essential practice for cloud-native API security. Rather than manually configuring infrastructure and services, security policies are codified and deployed alongside application code. Tools like Terraform, AWS CloudFormation, and Kubernetes manifests allow security teams to define access policies, network configurations, and resource constraints declaratively. These configurations can be versioned, peer-reviewed, and tested using automated pipelines, reducing the risk of misconfigurations and drift. Policy-as-code frameworks like Open Policy Agent further extend this approach by allowing the enforcement of fine-grained policies on API requests, deployments, and system states. These policies can prevent insecure configurations, such as deploying services without encryption or exposing privileged ports, before they reach production.

Secrets management is a persistent challenge in cloud-native API deployments. APIs often require credentials to access databases, third-party services, and internal systems. Hardcoding secrets into environment variables or configuration files exposes them to theft and misuse. Cloud-native platforms address this with dedicated secrets management services, such as AWS Secrets Manager, Azure Key Vault, and Google Secret Manager. These services provide encrypted storage, fine-grained access control, and automatic rotation. Secrets are injected at runtime using secure sidecar containers or platform APIs, ensuring they are never exposed to the build pipeline or stored in source code. Role-based access to secrets ensures that only the right workloads can retrieve specific credentials, further reducing the attack surface.

Cloud-native deployments often rely on CI/CD pipelines to build, test, and deploy APIs. Securing these pipelines is critical, as they control the entire lifecycle of the API infrastructure. Build pipelines must include security scanning steps such as static code analysis, dependency vulnerability detection, and container image validation. Tools like Trivy, Snyk, and SonarQube can be integrated to enforce quality gates. Signed container images and artifact verification provide guarantees that code has not been tampered with between build and deployment. Continuous validation of deployed infrastructure against security baselines ensures that runtime environments remain compliant and hardened against known risks.

In multi-cloud and hybrid environments, where APIs span across different cloud providers and on-premises systems, federation and consistency become major concerns. Identity federation allows services in one cloud to trust identities issued in another. This requires the use of open standards for authentication and the ability to verify tokens across providers. Cloud-native APIs must be designed to support cross-platform interoperability, consistent encryption, and unified logging across environments. Centralized policy engines and global control planes can help enforce consistent access control and monitoring rules, even in decentralized and federated architectures.

Security testing is vital in cloud-native API workflows. Traditional penetration testing must be supplemented with continuous automated testing to account for the pace and scale of deployments. Dynamic API scanners, fuzzers, and behavior-driven tests should be included in post-deployment stages to validate that APIs enforce correct permissions, handle malformed inputs safely, and conform to their expected behaviors. Shift-left security practices ensure that vulnerabilities are caught early in the development process, reducing the cost and risk of fixing them later. Teams must adopt a culture where security is a shared responsibility, embedded in every decision from design to deployment.

Cloud-native API security requires a holistic strategy that integrates identity, automation, visibility, and control across every layer of the stack. As services scale and evolve in real time, so too must the security practices that protect them. By leveraging cloud-native tools, adopting declarative security models, and embedding security into the software lifecycle, organizations can build resilient APIs that are protected against today's threats while remaining agile enough to adapt to tomorrow's challenges. The nature of cloud-native systems demands security approaches that are dynamic, scalable, and designed for constant change, ensuring that protection keeps pace with innovation.

# Securing APIs in Serverless Architectures

Serverless computing has introduced a paradigm shift in how applications and APIs are developed and deployed. In a serverless architecture, developers write and deploy code without managing the underlying infrastructure, allowing cloud providers to handle provisioning, scaling, and maintenance of servers. This model promotes agility, reduces operational overhead, and supports highly granular, event-driven execution. APIs built in serverless environments typically consist of cloud functions triggered by HTTP requests, messages, or events from other cloud services. While serverless architectures simplify development, they also introduce new and unique security challenges. Securing APIs in this context requires a tailored approach that addresses the ephemeral nature of functions, the reliance on managed services, and the need for fine-grained permissions and identity enforcement.

The ephemeral and stateless characteristics of serverless functions mean that traditional security mechanisms, such as long-lived sessions or persistent storage of tokens and logs, are not always applicable. Each function invocation is isolated and may run on a different instance or node than previous ones. As a result, any security context required by the function must be initialized at runtime and managed efficiently. Functions must authenticate incoming API requests using short-lived tokens or signatures that are validated with minimal delay. This makes the use of standard protocols like OAuth 2.0 and OpenID Connect particularly important. Tokens must be passed securely, verified promptly, and discarded after use, ensuring that no residual authentication artifacts are stored or leaked across invocations.

Authorization in serverless APIs must also be handled with precision. Since many serverless functions perform discrete tasks, each function should be granted the minimum necessary permissions to operate. This aligns with the principle of least privilege, which is crucial in preventing privilege escalation or lateral movement in the event of a compromised function. Cloud providers such as AWS, Azure, and Google Cloud allow fine-grained IAM policies to be attached to individual functions or roles. These policies define what actions a function can perform and what resources it can access. Overly permissive roles are a common security risk, so every function should be audited to ensure it only has the access required for its specific responsibilities.

API gateways in serverless architectures play a pivotal role in security. Most cloud platforms provide managed API gateway services that integrate seamlessly with serverless backends. These gateways handle TLS termination, request validation, authentication, and throttling. By offloading these responsibilities from the function itself, gateways provide a consistent and centralized layer of protection. Security policies enforced at the gateway level include CORS rules, IP whitelisting, request size limits, and the rejection of malformed requests. They also support integration with identity providers, enabling single sign-on and federated authentication for APIs that serve external users or third-party applications.

One of the significant risks in serverless API security is event injection. Since serverless functions can be triggered by various event sources, including storage events, messaging queues, and database changes, each of these sources becomes a potential vector for injection attacks. An attacker who gains control over a message queue or crafts a malicious event payload could trigger unexpected behavior in the function. To mitigate this, input validation and sanitization must be enforced rigorously, not only for HTTP inputs but for all event types. Functions should validate that inputs conform to expected schemas and reject any malformed or unexpected data. Employing schema validation libraries and runtime checks helps defend against injection attacks and logic abuse.

Another challenge in serverless security is managing secrets. Serverless functions often require access to API keys, database credentials, and other sensitive information. These secrets must never be hardcoded into the function code or passed in environment variables without encryption. Cloud-native secrets managers provide secure storage and access controls for managing credentials. Functions can retrieve secrets at runtime through secure APIs, with access governed by IAM policies. This allows secrets to be rotated regularly, audited, and revoked if necessary, without requiring redeployment of the function. The use of envelope encryption and hardware-backed key management services further enhances the protection of sensitive information.

Monitoring and logging are essential for detecting and responding to security incidents in serverless APIs. Due to the distributed and ephemeral nature of functions, collecting and correlating logs becomes more complex. Cloud providers typically offer centralized logging services that aggregate function logs, API gateway access logs, and platform-level events. These logs must be analyzed to detect anomalies such as unauthorized access attempts, high error rates, or unusual usage patterns. Real-time alerting, combined with automated incident response workflows, enables rapid containment and remediation. Serverless observability tools can trace the flow of a request across multiple functions and services, providing the visibility necessary to diagnose performance issues and investigate security events.

Rate limiting and abuse prevention are critical in serverless APIs, particularly because the model supports automatic scaling. While scalability is a benefit, it also means that an unprotected function can scale uncontrollably in response to malicious traffic, resulting in excessive resource consumption and financial cost. API gateways enforce rate limiting and throttling rules that restrict the number of requests per client or IP address. Additionally, usage quotas, request authentication, and user-level billing can discourage abuse. Serverless functions themselves should implement protective measures such as idempotency tokens, retry limits, and circuit breakers to guard against abuse of logic and backend dependencies.

Cold start behavior in serverless functions presents another security consideration. When a function is invoked for the first time or after a period of inactivity, it experiences a delay while the environment initializes. During this initialization, configuration files and dependencies are loaded into memory. Attackers may attempt to exploit predictable startup behavior or inject malicious content if the initialization phase includes unverified downloads or dynamic code loading. To minimize this risk, functions should use only trusted and verified packages, avoid downloading dependencies at runtime, and pre-warm instances where possible to reduce cold start exposure.

Serverless APIs also raise compliance concerns, particularly regarding data privacy and residency. Functions that process personal or regulated data must ensure that they do so in accordance with jurisdictional requirements. Data should be encrypted in transit and at rest, and audit logs must capture every access to sensitive information. Serverless platforms often provide regional deployment options, allowing functions to be hosted in specific geographic locations. Organizations must align their deployment strategies with data sovereignty laws and implement safeguards that prevent data from crossing unauthorized boundaries.

Secure deployment practices are vital in serverless environments. Continuous integration and deployment pipelines must include security testing stages such as static analysis, dependency vulnerability scanning, and policy enforcement. Infrastructure as code templates must be validated against security baselines to ensure that deployed functions have correct permissions, logging enabled, and monitoring configured. Version control, change tracking, and rollback mechanisms provide resilience against erroneous or malicious changes. Additionally, security reviews and threat modeling should be conducted regularly to assess the evolving risk landscape and adapt security strategies accordingly.

Securing APIs in serverless architectures requires a comprehensive strategy that embraces the unique characteristics of the serverless model. Identity-driven access, centralized gateways, strict permissions, secure secret handling, robust observability, and proactive governance are essential components. As serverless adoption continues to grow, security practices must evolve to address the challenges of scale, agility, and minimal operational control. By embedding security into every stage of the serverless lifecycle, from development to deployment to execution, organizations can harness the power of serverless computing without compromising the safety and integrity of their APIs.

# Static and Dynamic Analysis for API Code

Ensuring the security of API code requires a proactive and layered approach, beginning at the earliest stages of development and extending through deployment and runtime. Among the most effective techniques for identifying and mitigating vulnerabilities in API implementations are static and dynamic analysis. These methodologies offer distinct yet complementary perspectives on code security. Static analysis examines code without executing it, identifying flaws by inspecting source files, configuration files, or bytecode. Dynamic analysis, on the other hand, evaluates the behavior of an API while it is running, observing how the system responds to various inputs and environmental conditions. Together, these techniques enable comprehensive detection of weaknesses, reduce the attack surface, and improve the overall resilience of APIs against threats.

Static analysis is typically integrated into the development process, often as part of the continuous integration pipeline. It allows developers to identify potential vulnerabilities, coding errors, and deviations from security best practices before the application is even compiled or deployed. Tools that perform static application security testing, or SAST, scan the source code for patterns that indicate issues such as injection flaws, insecure data handling, improper error management, and misconfigured access controls. These tools can analyze code in multiple programming languages and are capable of tracing data flows across functions, modules, and even through third-party libraries to detect how untrusted input may traverse the application. For API code, this means examining the way request parameters are handled, how inputs are validated and sanitized, and whether sensitive data is adequately protected.

The power of static analysis lies in its ability to detect issues early, providing immediate feedback to developers and preventing vulnerable code from entering production environments. However, it also has limitations. Static analysis may produce false positives, flagging code that appears risky but is actually safe due to contextual logic not understood by the scanner. It may also struggle with certain dynamic behaviors or configurations that are determined at runtime. To overcome these limitations, static analysis results should be reviewed by developers or security engineers who understand the context and can determine whether findings are legitimate. High-quality tools often include rule customization, allowing teams to adjust sensitivity and focus on the most critical risks.

In contrast, dynamic analysis assesses the actual behavior of a running API. This involves sending crafted requests, observing responses, and monitoring how the API interacts with the underlying infrastructure, data stores, and external dependencies. Dynamic application security testing, or DAST, simulates attacks to identify issues that may not be visible through static inspection. These include logic flaws, authentication bypasses, session management problems, and misconfigurations. Dynamic analysis can be performed using automated tools that crawl the API, generate attack payloads, and assess the system's response for signs of vulnerability. These tools are particularly effective at identifying injection vulnerabilities, such as SQL injection or command injection, by analyzing how inputs affect outputs in real time.

Dynamic analysis provides insight into how an API behaves under real-world conditions, including how it handles malformed input, unusual request sequences, or unexpected data types. This form of testing is especially important for identifying vulnerabilities that emerge from the interaction between components, such as how an authentication service validates tokens or how a backend service parses JSON data. Because dynamic analysis observes the actual response of the system, it tends to produce fewer false positives than static analysis. However, it also has constraints. It can only evaluate the code paths that are exercised during testing, meaning that untested branches or hidden endpoints may remain unexamined. Furthermore, dynamic analysis requires a stable, running instance of the API and sufficient test coverage to be effective.

To maximize security, organizations should implement both static and dynamic analysis as part of a unified strategy. Static analysis should be used continuously during development, allowing developers to catch issues as they write code. Automated SAST scans triggered by each code commit or pull request provide rapid feedback and enforce coding standards. Dynamic analysis should be performed regularly in staging and pre-production environments, simulating real user behavior and malicious activity to uncover runtime issues. Integration of both types of analysis into CI/CD pipelines ensures that every deployment passes a security baseline check, and that vulnerabilities are addressed before reaching production.

In addition to traditional SAST and DAST tools, more advanced analysis techniques are emerging. Interactive Application Security Testing, or IAST, combines elements of both static and dynamic analysis by instrumenting the application and monitoring behavior during execution. This allows for highly accurate detection of vulnerabilities by observing how data flows through the application while it runs, in conjunction with source-level visibility. For APIs, IAST can reveal how specific request parameters influence internal state changes, how errors are handled across service boundaries, and whether access controls are enforced consistently.

Fuzz testing is another valuable dynamic technique where the API is bombarded with a wide range of unexpected or malformed inputs to observe how it reacts. This technique can expose crash conditions, unhandled exceptions, and other stability issues that might be exploited by attackers. In API environments, fuzzers are often configured to target specific endpoints and use knowledge of the API schema to generate more effective test cases. The combination of fuzzing with logging and observability tools provides deeper insights into the root causes of failures and guides developers toward more robust implementations.

Security analysis must also account for third-party dependencies and external APIs that the system relies on. Static analysis tools can scan dependency trees for known vulnerabilities using software composition analysis, or SCA. This helps detect risks introduced by outdated or compromised libraries, frameworks, and SDKs. Dynamic analysis tools can monitor calls to external APIs, assessing whether data is transmitted securely and whether proper authentication mechanisms are in place. By analyzing both the internal logic and external interactions, organizations gain a complete view of the security posture of their API ecosystems.

In modern development workflows, automation is key to achieving continuous and consistent analysis. Security tools must integrate with version control systems, build pipelines, and issue tracking platforms to create a seamless developer experience. Automated reports, actionable alerts, and remediation suggestions reduce the friction of security testing and encourage adoption across teams. Dashboards that visualize trends over time, identify recurring issues, and track progress toward compliance goals help prioritize efforts and demonstrate the effectiveness of security programs.

Static and dynamic analysis are essential components of any API security strategy. They address different phases of the development lifecycle, offer complementary insights, and support early detection of vulnerabilities. By embedding these practices into the development pipeline, organizations can catch risks before they become incidents, build more secure APIs, and foster a culture where security is an integral part of the software development process. As threats continue to evolve, the combination of static and dynamic analysis provides a robust foundation for defending against both known and emerging vulnerabilities.

# Secure API Design Patterns

Designing APIs with security at the forefront is essential in building robust, scalable, and trustworthy systems. As APIs continue to serve as the backbone of modern applications, powering everything from web and mobile interfaces to third-party integrations and internal microservices, the consequences of insecure design are more significant than ever. Security cannot be added as an afterthought. Instead, it must be embedded into the architecture from the beginning, following well-established design patterns that mitigate risk, reduce attack surfaces, and enable consistent enforcement of policies across environments. Secure API design patterns are practices and principles that guide developers in structuring APIs to resist common threats, preserve data confidentiality, and uphold system integrity.

One of the most critical aspects of secure API design is the consistent use of authentication mechanisms. APIs must clearly define how clients authenticate themselves and must ensure that every request includes sufficient credentials for validation. Token-based authentication, particularly using standards like OAuth 2.0 and OpenID Connect, is a widely adopted pattern that supports both user-centric and machine-to-machine access. APIs should be designed to expect and validate tokens on every request, using stateless verification where possible to reduce load on backend services. These tokens must be signed, short-lived, and scoped to specific actions to minimize the impact of token leakage or misuse. By enforcing strict authentication flows at the design level, APIs establish trust boundaries that can be relied upon consistently across deployments.

In addition to authentication, secure APIs must implement granular authorization logic. This means not only checking whether a user is authenticated but also verifying whether they are allowed to perform the requested action on the specific resource. Role-based access control is a foundational pattern, but in more dynamic environments, attribute-based or policy-based access control provides greater flexibility. The API design must include access checks at every level, especially for sensitive operations like modifying user data, triggering system changes, or accessing privileged endpoints. The principle of least privilege must guide the development of access rules, ensuring that users and systems are granted only the minimum necessary rights to complete their tasks.

Input validation is another foundational design pattern in secure APIs. Every input, whether from query parameters, headers, request bodies, or path variables, must be considered untrusted until validated. APIs should define strict schemas for input data, rejecting anything that deviates from the expected format. This includes enforcing type constraints, length limits, enumerated values, and structural requirements for complex objects. Schema validation libraries can automate much of this process, ensuring consistency and reducing developer error. Validating input at the boundary of the API helps prevent injection attacks, buffer overflows, and logic manipulation, all of which can be exploited by attackers to subvert application behavior.

Output encoding and response consistency also play a significant role in secure API design. APIs must never expose sensitive internal information in error messages, responses, or logs. This includes stack traces, database queries, configuration details, or user-specific identifiers that could aid an attacker. Standardized error responses should be used across the API, providing enough information for clients to debug issues without revealing the internal workings of the system. Encoding output before rendering it in a browser or including it in a response body ensures that injection payloads are not executed inadvertently, mitigating risks such as cross-site scripting when APIs are consumed by web clients.

Rate limiting is a design pattern that protects APIs from abuse and denial-of-service attacks. By limiting the number of requests a client can make over a given period, APIs can enforce fair usage, prevent resource exhaustion, and mitigate brute-force attacks. Rate limits should be applied per user, per token, per IP address, or per endpoint depending on the context. The design must define what happens when limits are exceeded, typically returning a standardized HTTP 429 response with headers indicating the retry window. When implemented correctly, rate limiting acts as both a protective measure and a signal to clients to adjust their behavior.

Secure APIs also follow a pattern of using HTTPS exclusively. All communication between clients and servers must be encrypted using strong TLS configurations to protect against eavesdropping, tampering, and man-in-the-middle attacks. The design must ensure that all endpoints enforce HTTPS and redirect any HTTP traffic accordingly. Additionally, APIs should adopt mechanisms such as HSTS to instruct browsers and clients to always use encrypted connections. Secure transport is a non-negotiable baseline for any modern API and must be enforced without exception.

Versioning is another area where secure design plays a role. APIs should clearly define versioning strategies to avoid breaking changes that could lead clients to misuse new or deprecated functionality. Path-based versioning is a common pattern, making it clear which version of the API is in use. When versions are deprecated, the API must provide a clear migration path and maintain security controls across all active versions. Abandoning older versions without properly managing access controls can lead to unmaintained surfaces vulnerable to attack.

Idempotency is a secure design principle particularly relevant to write operations. By ensuring that certain operations can be repeated safely without unintended side effects, APIs reduce the risk of duplicate actions caused by retries or malicious requests. For instance, POST operations for resource creation can include idempotency keys that ensure only one instance of the operation is executed. This pattern helps prevent issues such as duplicate payments, data corruption, or inconsistent state changes, improving both reliability and security.

Another critical design consideration is logging and observability. Secure APIs must log all access attempts, errors, and security-relevant events such as failed authentication or permission denials. However, care must be taken to avoid logging sensitive data such as passwords, tokens, or personally identifiable information. Logs must be structured, tamper-resistant, and integrated into monitoring systems that support alerting and auditing. Observability patterns, including the use of request identifiers, correlation IDs, and distributed tracing, allow security teams to track interactions across services, detect anomalies, and investigate incidents with precision.

Secure API design must also address dependency management. APIs often rely on third-party libraries, SDKs, or external APIs. These dependencies must be carefully vetted, updated regularly, and scanned for vulnerabilities. The design must account for the possibility that an upstream dependency could introduce security flaws, and strategies such as dependency pinning, integrity verification, and sandboxing must be considered. Keeping a minimal and trusted set of dependencies reduces the likelihood of indirect compromise and supports more maintainable security practices.

Finally, documentation and developer experience are vital elements of secure API design. Clear, complete, and accurate documentation ensures that developers understand how to interact with the API securely. This includes guidance on authentication flows, permission scopes, input formats, rate limits, and error handling. By promoting secure usage patterns through well-written documentation, APIs reduce the chance of accidental misconfigurations or security oversights by client developers. Secure defaults, helpful error messages, and client libraries that enforce best practices further reinforce the correct use of the API.

Secure API design patterns provide a structured framework for building resilient, trustworthy interfaces that can withstand the evolving threat landscape. By embedding these patterns into every layer of the API, from transport to logic to behavior, developers create systems that not only perform well but also uphold the highest standards of security. These patterns serve as a blueprint for sustainable and scalable development, ensuring that as APIs grow and evolve, their security posture remains strong and adaptive.

# API Security Incident Response Planning

Planning for security incidents is a fundamental responsibility for any organization that operates APIs, particularly as these interfaces become the primary vector for application access, data exchange, and third-party integration. APIs are attractive targets for attackers due to the sensitive data they expose and the powerful operations they often perform. Whether the threat involves data breaches, token theft, denial-of-service attacks, or abuse of business logic, the speed and effectiveness of an organization's response can determine the scope and severity of the impact. API security incident response planning is the structured process of preparing for, detecting, responding to, and recovering from security incidents that affect API infrastructure. A comprehensive response plan must be aligned with the organization's overall cybersecurity strategy but tailored specifically to the unique characteristics of API environments.

The foundation of any incident response plan is preparation. This includes defining what constitutes a security incident in the context of APIs. An incident could be an unauthorized access attempt, an unexpected spike in API traffic, suspicious behavior from a known client, a known vulnerability being exploited, or a breach involving exposed data. These scenarios must be clearly documented, and incident categories must be assigned based on severity and potential impact. Preparation also involves assembling a cross-functional response team that includes members from security, development, operations, and legal departments. Each member must understand their roles and responsibilities and be trained regularly on the procedures and tools used during an incident.

Preparation further extends to establishing monitoring and alerting systems capable of detecting abnormal API activity in real time. Logs must be collected and stored centrally with proper access controls to ensure they are available and tamper-evident. Logs should capture request metadata such as IP addresses, tokens, endpoints accessed, and response codes. Alerting mechanisms must be configured to trigger notifications when predefined thresholds or suspicious patterns are observed, such as repeated failed logins, access to deprecated endpoints, or unusual data transfer volumes. These alerts must integrate with incident management systems to automatically assign priority levels and initiate response workflows.

Once an alert is generated, the detection phase begins. The response team must confirm whether the alert represents a true incident or a false positive. This involves correlating information from logs, monitoring dashboards, authentication systems, and threat intelligence feeds. The team must determine the scope of the incident, including which APIs were affected, which users or systems were involved, what data may have been exposed, and whether the incident is ongoing or has already ended. Rapid and accurate detection is essential to minimizing damage, especially when incidents involve automated attacks that can exfiltrate data or cause service disruption within minutes.

The next phase is containment. The goal here is to limit the spread and impact of the incident while preserving forensic evidence for investigation. Containment strategies vary depending on the type of incident. In the case of token theft, the affected tokens must be revoked, and the associated sessions terminated. If an API key has been compromised, the key must be disabled, and the client must be notified to generate a new one. For abuse of specific endpoints, rate limits or access control rules may need to be adjusted to block the offending traffic. In more severe cases, the API gateway may need to redirect or drop requests from specific IP ranges or regions. All containment actions must be logged and approved according to predefined policies to ensure consistency and accountability.

After containment is achieved, the team moves into the eradication and recovery phase. This involves identifying and removing the root cause of the incident, such as a misconfigured access control, a vulnerable dependency, or a logic flaw in the API code. If necessary, the affected API components must be patched, reconfigured, or redeployed. Once the root cause is addressed, services can be restored to normal operation in a controlled and monitored manner. Any data that was corrupted or lost during the incident must be restored from secure backups. Clients and users impacted by the incident must be notified with accurate and timely information, following regulatory disclosure requirements where applicable.

Throughout the entire incident response process, documentation is critical. Every action taken, from the initial alert to the final resolution, must be recorded in an incident log. This includes timestamps, responsible personnel, evidence gathered, and decisions made. These records serve not only for compliance and audit purposes but also for the post-incident analysis that follows recovery. Once the incident is resolved, a thorough review must be conducted to evaluate what went wrong, what was done correctly, and what improvements can be made. This retrospective should include a root cause analysis, a timeline of events, an assessment of the response effectiveness, and a set of actionable recommendations for strengthening defenses.

Incident response planning for APIs must also consider legal and regulatory obligations. Depending on the nature of the data processed by the API and the jurisdictions in which it operates, certain disclosures may be required within a specific timeframe. The plan must outline how legal counsel will be engaged, how evidence will be preserved for potential investigations, and how communication with stakeholders will be managed. Public relations teams may also need to be involved in messaging to customers, partners, or the media. The ability to respond confidently and transparently to a public breach can significantly influence the long-term reputation and trustworthiness of the organization.

Automation plays a growing role in incident response for API environments. Given the speed and scale of modern threats, automated tools must be used to detect anomalies, correlate alerts, initiate containment actions, and support investigation workflows. Security orchestration platforms can integrate multiple systems, triggering predefined playbooks based on incident type and severity. For example, when an anomaly is detected in token usage patterns, an automated workflow can immediately revoke the token, notify the user, and escalate the case to a human analyst for further review. These automated responses not only reduce reaction time but also ensure that incidents are handled consistently and according to policy.

Ongoing testing and simulation are essential to ensure the effectiveness of the incident response plan. Regular tabletop exercises, red team engagements, and simulated breaches allow the response team to practice their procedures, identify gaps, and build muscle memory for high-stress situations. These exercises must include API-specific scenarios such as credential stuffing attacks, unauthorized access to a protected endpoint, or exploitation of a deserialization vulnerability. The findings from these drills should be used to update the response plan, refine tooling, and improve training.

API security incident response planning is not a static document or a one-time exercise. It is a living strategy that must evolve with the API landscape, the threat environment, and the technological infrastructure of the organization. As APIs grow in number, complexity, and importance, so too does the need for a well-coordinated and proactive approach to managing security incidents. With the right planning, tools, and training in place, organizations can not only minimize the damage caused by incidents but also emerge stronger, more resilient, and better prepared for the future.


# Regulatory Compliance for API Security

Regulatory compliance is a critical dimension of API security, especially in industries and regions where data protection and privacy are enforced by law. As APIs increasingly become the primary means of accessing and exchanging sensitive data, including personal information, financial transactions, and healthcare records, organizations must ensure that their API implementations conform to the standards and obligations imposed by global regulations. Failing to meet these requirements can result in severe consequences, including financial penalties, legal action, operational restrictions, and reputational damage. Therefore, designing and managing APIs with compliance in mind is not just a matter of best practice but a fundamental business necessity.

The growing number of data protection laws across different jurisdictions has made compliance a complex and dynamic challenge. Regulations such as the General Data Protection Regulation in the European Union, the Health Insurance Portability and Accountability Act in the United States, the California Consumer Privacy Act, and the Payment Card Industry Data Security Standard each impose specific expectations around data handling, access control, auditing, and breach notification. These expectations directly impact how APIs are designed, deployed, and secured. API providers must be able to demonstrate that their interfaces do not inadvertently expose regulated data, allow unauthorized access, or fail to log and retain evidence of activity.

One of the foundational requirements of most regulatory frameworks is the protection of personal data. APIs that handle personally identifiable information must enforce strong authentication and authorization mechanisms to ensure that only authorized users and systems can access such data. Token-based authentication with scopes, claims, and expiration is essential to restrict access to the appropriate parties. APIs must also implement fine-grained access controls, verifying not only the identity of the requester but also their entitlement to access a specific resource or perform a particular action. For example, in healthcare applications governed by HIPAA, access to medical records must be granted only to individuals with a documented clinical need, and every access attempt must be logged and reviewed.

Data minimization is another key principle enforced by regulations like GDPR and CCPA. APIs must be designed to expose only the necessary data required for the operation or transaction. This involves carefully controlling the structure of API responses, avoiding overexposure through verbose payloads, and implementing filtering mechanisms that allow clients to request only the fields they need. Excessive data exposure not only increases the attack surface but also violates the principle of collecting and sharing only what is necessary. Developers must ensure that debug endpoints, deprecated versions, and undocumented features do not inadvertently leak sensitive information that could trigger regulatory scrutiny.

Encryption plays a major role in ensuring compliance. APIs must use encryption to protect data both in transit and at rest. For data in transit, secure communication protocols such as HTTPS with TLS must be enforced without exception. Certificate management must be automated and monitored to prevent the use of expired or invalid certificates. For data at rest, cloud storage, databases, and backups must implement strong encryption mechanisms, often supported by hardware security modules or cloud-native key management services. Access to encryption keys must be tightly controlled and audited, with automatic rotation schedules and revocation processes in place.

Auditability is a requirement in virtually all compliance frameworks. APIs must produce logs that capture the who, what, when, and where of each interaction. These logs must include the identity of the user or service making the request, the resource accessed, the action performed, the time of the request, and the result. Logs must be tamper-resistant, encrypted, and retained for a period defined by the applicable regulation. For example, PCI DSS requires that logs be preserved for at least one year and that the most recent three months be immediately available for analysis. APIs must integrate with centralized logging platforms that support secure storage, indexing, alerting, and reporting to support compliance audits and incident investigations.

Consent management is another critical area in regulatory compliance. APIs that process personal data must support the capture, verification, and enforcement of user consent. This means that before collecting or processing data, the API must verify that consent has been granted, and it must allow users to withdraw consent at any time. The consent mechanism must be explicit, informed, and freely given. In the context of APIs, this often requires integration with consent management platforms and the inclusion of consent tokens or flags in API requests and responses. APIs must respond appropriately when consent is revoked, including deleting or anonymizing data as required by the data subject's request.

Breach notification requirements impose strict timelines and processes for responding to data leaks or unauthorized access. APIs must be monitored continuously for signs of compromise, including unusual traffic patterns, failed login attempts, or access to restricted endpoints. When a breach is detected, the organization must be able to determine the scope of the impact, identify affected individuals, and notify regulators and users within a specific timeframe, often seventy-two hours or less. APIs must be instrumented with monitoring and alerting tools that can detect, log, and escalate incidents in real time, enabling the organization to respond swiftly and in compliance with legal obligations.

Cross-border data transfer is another regulatory consideration that affects API design. Some regulations restrict the movement of personal data outside certain geographic boundaries unless adequate protections are in place. APIs that handle such data must verify the location of the requesting client, determine the residency of the data, and enforce restrictions accordingly. This may involve deploying regional API endpoints, using geofencing, or encrypting data in such a way that it can only be decrypted within an approved jurisdiction. Cloud providers often offer regional services and compliance features to assist with these requirements, but the responsibility for proper configuration lies with the API provider.

Compliance also involves transparency. API providers must publish clear documentation that explains what data is collected, how it is processed, and who has access to it. Privacy policies must align with actual API behavior, and discrepancies between stated policies and implemented logic can lead to legal exposure. Developers must ensure that API documentation is accurate, updated regularly, and aligned with the regulatory disclosures required for their jurisdiction. Tools that automate documentation generation from API definitions can help ensure consistency and reduce the risk of miscommunication.

Maintaining regulatory compliance is an ongoing process, not a one-time certification. As regulations evolve, so must the security controls and practices embedded in API infrastructure. Regular audits, both internal and external, must be conducted to verify that controls are functioning as intended. Vulnerability assessments, penetration testing, and compliance checklists must be used to identify gaps and track remediation progress. Training and awareness programs must be conducted to ensure that all stakeholders, from developers to legal teams, understand their roles in maintaining compliance. Automation can help enforce compliance policies through continuous integration pipelines, security-as-code practices, and policy-based deployment controls.

Regulatory compliance for API security is a multi-dimensional challenge that requires attention to technical, procedural, and legal details. By integrating compliance requirements into the design, development, and deployment of APIs, organizations not only meet their legal obligations but also build more trustworthy, resilient, and transparent systems. As the regulatory landscape continues to evolve and expand, a proactive and comprehensive approach to compliance becomes an indispensable part of any API security strategy.

# GDPR and Data Minimization in API Design

The General Data Protection Regulation, known as GDPR, has had a profound impact on the design and operation of APIs, particularly those that handle personal data. Enacted by the European Union, GDPR mandates strict rules for the collection, processing, storage, and transfer of personal information related to individuals within the EU. One of the central tenets of the regulation is the principle of data minimization, which requires that only the minimum necessary personal data be collected and processed for any given purpose. For API developers and architects, this principle demands a fundamental shift in how APIs are structured, what data they expose, how access is granted, and how data flows are managed throughout the system lifecycle.

Data minimization begins with intentional and thoughtful API schema design. When creating API endpoints that accept input or return data, the payload structure must be carefully evaluated to ensure that only the data strictly required for the operation is present. This means avoiding the temptation to return entire user objects or datasets when only a subset of fields is needed. For instance, if an endpoint returns user information for profile display, it should not include unnecessary internal identifiers, historical metadata, or contact information unless the client explicitly requires it and is authorized to view it. Each field in the API response must be justified by a legitimate business purpose aligned with user expectations and data protection laws.

To enforce data minimization in practice, APIs must support selective data retrieval mechanisms. This can be achieved through query parameters that allow clients to specify which fields they need, or through the use of well-defined data projection schemas. By supporting fine-grained data access, APIs reduce the exposure of unnecessary personal information and minimize the risk of leaks, breaches, or misuse. Furthermore, APIs should reject or flag requests that attempt to access data beyond what is needed or permitted. This not only aligns with GDPR but also improves performance and reduces bandwidth consumption.

Another key aspect of GDPR compliance is purpose limitation. APIs must not only collect minimal data but also ensure that the data is used only for the specific purpose stated at the time of collection. This requires tight coupling between API functionality and consent management. Whenever an API is invoked to collect or process user data, it must verify that appropriate consent has been obtained and that the requested operation falls within the scope of that consent. Consent should be granular, revocable, and clearly documented. APIs must integrate with consent management systems that track which users have consented to which purposes and update that information in real time. If consent is withdrawn, APIs must cease further processing of that data and, where appropriate, delete or anonymize it.

The GDPR also enshrines the right to access, rectification, and erasure of personal data. These rights must be reflected in API capabilities. Users must be able to retrieve all personal data held about them, correct inaccuracies, and request deletion where applicable. This requires APIs to expose secure, authenticated endpoints that return complete and comprehensible data sets to data subjects upon request. The design of these endpoints must prevent unauthorized access, ensure auditability, and return only the data relevant to the authenticated user. Implementing these features involves robust identity verification, access controls, and logging mechanisms to ensure that responses are traceable, secure, and compliant with legal standards.

Anonymization and pseudonymization are techniques strongly encouraged by GDPR, particularly in scenarios where data must be processed without identifying individuals. APIs that support analytics, logging, or third-party integrations should remove or mask personal identifiers unless absolutely necessary. For example, logs should not store full user names, email addresses, or IP addresses unless required for debugging or compliance purposes. Where personal data is needed temporarily, APIs must implement mechanisms to purge or obfuscate that data after its purpose is fulfilled. Pseudonymized data can allow valuable insights to be drawn without exposing real identities, thereby reducing the risk in the event of a breach.

Security and encryption are also essential to ensuring data minimization is upheld. GDPR requires that organizations implement appropriate technical measures to protect personal data from unauthorized access, alteration, or destruction. For API traffic, this means enforcing HTTPS for all communications, verifying TLS certificates, and employing strong cipher suites. Sensitive data transmitted via API requests or responses must be encrypted both in transit and at rest. Encryption keys must be managed securely and rotated regularly. Moreover, sensitive operations within APIs, such as account creation, login, or financial transactions, must be guarded with multi-factor authentication and rate limiting to prevent abuse.

Data retention policies must be encoded into API logic to comply with GDPR's requirement that personal data not be stored longer than necessary. This means that APIs responsible for storing or accessing user data must be aware of data retention timelines and automatically delete or archive data that has reached the end of its lifecycle. Data expiration policies should be enforced using scheduled tasks or event-driven functions that regularly clean up outdated records. Clients interacting with such APIs should be made aware of these timelines to avoid confusion or loss of functionality. The API's documentation must clearly explain how long data is retained, what triggers its deletion, and how users can influence those settings.

Cross-border data transfers are another critical area governed by GDPR. APIs that transmit personal data to locations outside the European Economic Area must ensure that the receiving country has adequate data protection measures in place. This may involve using standard contractual clauses, binding corporate rules, or other legal mechanisms approved by regulators. The API must verify the location of the requesting client and enforce transfer restrictions where required. Additionally, APIs must log and audit all such transfers to demonstrate compliance and support future investigations or data subject requests.

API developers must also consider the accountability principle under GDPR. Organizations are required to demonstrate that they are meeting their obligations through documentation, monitoring, and continuous improvement. For APIs, this means maintaining thorough documentation of data flows, privacy impact assessments, security controls, and access policies. APIs should expose telemetry and audit trails that show how personal data is being processed, by whom, and for what purpose. Regular reviews, internal audits, and third-party assessments help ensure that APIs continue to align with evolving regulatory standards and best practices.

The implementation of GDPR and data minimization principles in API design is not just a legal obligation but a critical component of building user trust and safeguarding organizational reputation. By designing APIs that collect less data, process it with clear intent, and protect it with strong controls, organizations create digital systems that are resilient, respectful, and compliant with modern data protection values. As more jurisdictions adopt privacy laws modeled after GDPR, the ability to integrate data minimization into the core of API architecture will define the future of responsible software development and user-centric innovation.

# PCI DSS Considerations for APIs

The Payment Card Industry Data Security Standard, or PCI DSS, establishes comprehensive security requirements for organizations that store, process, or transmit payment card information. APIs, as conduits for financial data in modern applications, are subject to these standards whenever they handle cardholder data, even indirectly. With the widespread use of APIs in e-commerce platforms, mobile payment apps, and digital banking services, ensuring that APIs are PCI DSS compliant is essential not only for avoiding penalties and fines but also for maintaining the integrity of the payment ecosystem. Compliance with PCI DSS for APIs requires meticulous attention to authentication, encryption, logging, access control, and architectural segmentation to minimize risk and ensure that sensitive cardholder data remains protected at all times.

One of the core principles of PCI DSS is the protection of cardholder data during transmission across open, public networks. APIs must enforce strong transport encryption using current and secure versions of the TLS protocol. The use of outdated or deprecated encryption protocols, such as SSL or early versions of TLS, is strictly prohibited. APIs must reject insecure connections and enforce the use of secure ciphers. Certificates must be issued by a trusted certificate authority and managed to ensure they are not expired or revoked. In addition to TLS, all communication involving cardholder data must be validated for integrity to prevent tampering, and client-server authentication must be rigorously implemented to prevent man-in-the-middle attacks.

Encryption alone is not sufficient. PCI DSS also requires that only the minimum necessary cardholder data be transmitted or exposed. This aligns with broader security and privacy principles such as data minimization. API responses must be carefully constructed to exclude unnecessary data elements. For instance, if a transaction confirmation does not require the full primary account number, that number must be truncated or omitted. The same applies to expiration dates, CVV codes, and track data, which must never be stored post-authorization and must not be accessible through API endpoints unless specifically justified. APIs must be designed to limit the scope of cardholder data exposure and to prevent inadvertent logging or caching of sensitive information.

Access control is another central pillar of PCI DSS. APIs must ensure that only authorized users and systems have access to cardholder data and that each access attempt is authenticated, logged, and evaluated against predefined roles and permissions. Role-based access control must be implemented to ensure that users are granted only the privileges necessary for their role. Strong authentication mechanisms must be used for all API consumers, including multi-factor authentication for administrative or privileged accounts. In environments where API access is automated, as with server-to-server communication, credentials must be stored securely, rotated regularly, and revoked when no longer needed.

Authentication tokens, API keys, and session identifiers must be protected with the same rigor as cardholder data. They must be transmitted only over secure channels, stored in encrypted formats, and never exposed in logs, URLs, or error messages. Tokens must have short expiration times and must be scoped to specific resources and operations. Systems must monitor for signs of credential abuse or anomalies in access patterns, which could indicate a compromised account. The use of shared credentials must be avoided, and each system or user must have a unique identifier to support detailed auditing and traceability.

PCI DSS mandates robust logging and monitoring of all access to systems handling cardholder data. APIs must produce logs that detail access events, including the identity of the requester, the resource accessed, the action performed, the time of the event, and the result. These logs must be stored securely, protected against tampering, and retained for at least one year, with at least three months immediately available for analysis. APIs must integrate with centralized logging systems that support correlation, alerting, and forensic analysis. In the event of suspicious activity or a potential breach, logs serve as the primary source of evidence and must be reliable and comprehensive.

API endpoints must also be subject to regular vulnerability assessments and penetration testing as required by PCI DSS. These tests must be conducted by qualified personnel and should target both known vulnerabilities and business logic flaws. Automated scanning tools should be used to detect issues such as injection vulnerabilities, insecure configurations, and exposed endpoints. In addition to periodic scans, APIs must be tested after significant changes such as code updates, infrastructure changes, or new integrations. Identified vulnerabilities must be remediated promptly and tracked to resolution, and compensating controls must be documented if immediate remediation is not feasible.

Another important consideration is network segmentation. APIs that process or expose cardholder data must be logically and physically separated from non-sensitive systems. This segmentation limits the scope of PCI DSS compliance and reduces the attack surface. Firewalls, reverse proxies, and API gateways must be configured to strictly control inbound and outbound traffic to and from the cardholder data environment. Only necessary communication paths should be permitted, and all other traffic must be denied by default. Access to API endpoints should be restricted to authorized IP addresses, services, or cloud identities. Service meshes and container orchestration platforms must enforce service-to-service communication policies to prevent unauthorized lateral movement within the infrastructure.

Secure development practices are essential for maintaining PCI DSS compliance throughout the API lifecycle. APIs must be developed using secure coding techniques that prevent common vulnerabilities such as cross-site scripting, SQL injection, command injection, and improper error handling. Static application security testing must be integrated into the development pipeline to catch issues early. Secure code reviews, peer audits, and threat modeling exercises must be conducted regularly. Development, testing, and production environments must be segregated to prevent data leakage and unauthorized access. Test data must never include real cardholder data, and development endpoints must not expose sensitive functionality.

Incident response planning is also a required component of PCI DSS and must include specific provisions for APIs. In the event of a data breach or attempted attack involving APIs, the organization must be able to detect the incident, contain it, assess its impact, and notify relevant stakeholders within regulatory timelines. This requires integration between API monitoring tools, security information and event management systems, and the organization's broader incident response framework. Staff must be trained to recognize indicators of compromise and to execute predefined playbooks to minimize damage and support recovery.

Maintaining PCI DSS compliance for APIs is not a one-time task but an ongoing process that must evolve with changes in technology, threat landscapes, and business requirements. Continuous compliance monitoring, regular training, and automated enforcement of security policies help ensure that APIs remain secure and auditable. As APIs continue to handle increasing volumes of financial data, their role in achieving and maintaining PCI DSS compliance becomes ever more critical. By integrating security into every stage of the API lifecycle and aligning practices with PCI DSS requirements, organizations can protect payment data, support customer trust, and avoid the operational and financial consequences of non-compliance.

# API Security in Mobile App Backends

Mobile applications rely heavily on backend APIs to perform essential functions such as user authentication, data synchronization, content delivery, and transaction processing. These APIs form the bridge between the mobile client and the backend systems that host data and business logic. However, their exposure to the public internet and the predictable nature of mobile traffic patterns make them attractive targets for malicious actors. Securing APIs that serve mobile apps requires a distinct set of considerations, accounting for both the unique behavior of mobile environments and the common threats associated with remote interfaces. Robust API security in this context demands careful design, vigilant monitoring, and layered defenses to ensure that sensitive data and critical services are protected.

One of the most common mistakes in mobile backend security is assuming that the mobile app itself is secure and cannot be tampered with. In reality, mobile applications are distributed to end-user devices where attackers can reverse-engineer them, inspect the code, modify functionality, and extract sensitive information such as API keys or hardcoded credentials. Therefore, any security measure that depends solely on the secrecy or integrity of the mobile application should be considered weak. API backends must treat all requests from mobile clients as potentially untrusted and enforce server-side security policies independently of any validation performed on the client side.

Authentication and authorization mechanisms must be carefully implemented to validate the identity and permissions of mobile app users. Token-based authentication using OAuth 2.0 is widely adopted in mobile environments. The mobile app authenticates the user through a secure login process and receives an access token, which is then included in subsequent API requests. These tokens should be short-lived and refreshed frequently to limit exposure in the event of token compromise. Refresh tokens must be stored securely, and any abnormal usage patterns, such as token replay or use from multiple devices, should trigger alerts or additional verification steps. Mobile backends must verify the token signature, expiration, audience, and scope on every request to ensure that access is granted only to authenticated users with appropriate permissions.

Transport security is another critical layer. All communication between the mobile app and the API backend must be encrypted using HTTPS with TLS. API endpoints must enforce HTTPS strictly, redirecting or rejecting any plaintext HTTP requests. Certificates must be issued by a trusted authority and validated by the client application. In addition, mobile apps can implement certificate pinning to ensure they only trust a specific certificate or public key, reducing the risk of man-in-the-middle attacks. However, certificate pinning must be implemented with care to avoid breaking connectivity during certificate renewals or rotations.

Rate limiting and throttling are essential to protect mobile APIs from abuse. Attackers may attempt to brute-force authentication, scrape data, or exhaust system resources using automated tools that mimic mobile traffic. API gateways or backend services must enforce per-user and per-IP rate limits to restrict the number of requests that can be made within a given time frame. Limits should be configurable based on endpoint sensitivity and the type of operation being performed. Responses to rate-limited clients must include clear headers indicating the limit, remaining quota, and reset time to support graceful client-side behavior.

Input validation and sanitization must be applied rigorously to all incoming data from mobile apps. Mobile clients can be manipulated to send malformed or malicious data, exploiting vulnerabilities such as injection attacks, buffer overflows, or logic flaws. APIs must define strict schemas for request bodies, query parameters, and headers, and validate every field for type, format, length, and acceptable values. Any deviation from the expected format should result in a rejection of the request with a clear and safe error message. Validation should be implemented server-side using trusted libraries and frameworks to prevent inconsistencies or bypasses.

Mobile backends must also address session management and device identification. Sessions associated with mobile users must be tied to specific devices or contexts to prevent hijacking. Device identifiers, while useful, must not be relied upon as secure authentication factors due to their susceptibility to spoofing. Instead, mobile apps should establish unique installation identifiers combined with secure key storage and cryptographic attestation techniques. Backend systems should track login activity, session duration, and device fingerprinting data to detect anomalies such as logins from multiple locations or sudden changes in device attributes.

Data minimization is a best practice that supports both security and privacy. APIs should return only the data that is necessary for a given operation, avoiding overexposure of user details, configuration values, or internal metadata. Responses should be tailored to the user's role and current session context. For example, a standard user querying their account information should not receive fields that are only relevant to administrators or internal systems. Error messages must also be designed to avoid leaking sensitive information. Generic messages such as unauthorized or bad request should replace detailed stack traces or configuration hints that could aid an attacker in reconnaissance.

Monitoring and logging are indispensable components of a secure mobile API backend. Every request must be logged with metadata such as timestamp, user identifier, IP address, endpoint accessed, and response code. These logs must be stored securely and analyzed in real-time to detect suspicious patterns such as excessive failed logins, access from unusual geolocations, or sudden spikes in traffic volume. Integration with security information and event management platforms allows for correlation across systems and supports rapid response to emerging threats. In addition, backend systems should support audit trails for sensitive operations such as data modifications, payment processing, or changes in user permissions.

Third-party SDKs and libraries used by mobile apps can introduce additional risks to backend APIs. Many SDKs communicate directly with backend services or relay requests from the app. Developers must vet all third-party components for security, monitor them for vulnerabilities, and restrict their access to only the API endpoints required for their function. Backend APIs must not trust requests simply because they originate from a known SDK or platform component. All requests must be subject to the same authentication, authorization, and validation controls as those initiated directly by the mobile application.

Finally, a secure deployment and update process is essential to maintaining API security in mobile app backends. Changes to the API must be tested for regressions, security flaws, and compatibility with deployed mobile clients. Versioning strategies must be in place to allow clients to migrate gradually and safely. Backward compatibility must be balanced with the need to deprecate insecure or obsolete functionality. When security patches are deployed, mechanisms must be in place to revoke affected tokens, invalidate compromised sessions, and notify users or administrators of required actions. Security must also be embedded into the software development lifecycle, with automated tests, peer reviews, and continuous integration tools enforcing best practices at every stage.

Securing APIs in mobile app backends requires a holistic approach that addresses the client-server boundary, defends against common threats, and enforces strong identity and data protections. As mobile usage continues to rise and applications handle increasingly sensitive data and transactions, the API backend becomes a critical security frontier. By implementing layered defenses, continuous monitoring, and secure design principles, developers can ensure that their mobile APIs remain resilient in the face of evolving risks and adversaries.

# IoT and API Security Challenges

The explosive growth of the Internet of Things has introduced a vast and complex ecosystem of interconnected devices, many of which rely on APIs to send and receive data, interact with cloud platforms, and execute remote commands. From consumer-grade smart home products to industrial sensors and critical infrastructure controls, IoT devices are increasingly dependent on APIs for real-time communication and management. While APIs provide the flexibility and interoperability that IoT architectures require, they also expose significant security challenges. These challenges stem from the distributed and often insecure nature of IoT devices, the scale and heterogeneity of deployments, and the difficulty of applying traditional security models to constrained environments. Securing APIs in the IoT context requires a deep understanding of the unique threat landscape, architectural constraints, and operational limitations associated with embedded systems and device-to-cloud communication.

One of the most prominent challenges in IoT API security is device authentication. In conventional web or mobile environments, users authenticate themselves using credentials, tokens, or biometric identifiers. In contrast, IoT devices are typically autonomous, headless, and operate without human intervention. This means that device identity must be established and maintained through automated and tamper-resistant means. Devices often ship with hardcoded credentials or shared keys, which can be easily extracted through reverse engineering or physical tampering. Once compromised, these credentials can be used to impersonate devices, send false data, or issue malicious commands. A more secure approach involves provisioning each device with a unique identity, typically using X.509 certificates or hardware-based trusted platform modules. Mutual TLS can then be used to authenticate both the device and the server, ensuring that each side of the connection is verified before data is exchanged.

Another significant issue is the lack of standardization across IoT platforms and device manufacturers. Many IoT devices implement proprietary protocols, undocumented APIs, or minimal security features due to cost or resource constraints. This fragmentation makes it difficult to establish uniform security policies or perform consistent vulnerability assessments. APIs exposed by devices may lack proper authentication, fail to validate inputs, or transmit sensitive data in plaintext. In such environments, attackers can exploit poorly secured endpoints to gain unauthorized access, extract data, or disrupt operations. This problem is compounded by the fact that many IoT deployments are long-lived, with devices remaining in operation for years without firmware updates or security patches. APIs designed for such environments must anticipate long-term exposure and minimize reliance on client-side controls.

Data integrity and confidentiality are critical concerns in IoT API communication. Devices often transmit sensor readings, location data, or operational metrics that inform downstream decisions. If this data is intercepted, altered, or spoofed, it can lead to incorrect actions, safety hazards, or operational failures. For example, a smart thermostat receiving manipulated temperature data may activate heating or cooling unnecessarily, wasting energy and causing discomfort. To prevent such scenarios, API communication must be encrypted end-to-end, and payloads must be validated using cryptographic signatures or checksums. Lightweight cryptographic algorithms must be used for constrained devices to ensure security without exhausting computational or power resources. Additionally, APIs must enforce rate limits and anomaly detection to identify and block suspicious patterns such as repeated failed authentications or large bursts of unexpected traffic.

IoT devices also pose a unique challenge in terms of lifecycle management. From manufacturing to deployment, and from operation to decommissioning, each stage introduces opportunities for API misuse or security lapses. During initial provisioning, APIs must ensure that devices are registered securely, avoiding replay attacks or unauthorized enrollment. Once operational, devices must regularly authenticate with backend APIs, refresh credentials, and verify firmware integrity. Any lapse in this process can create a foothold for attackers. When devices are decommissioned, their associated API tokens or credentials must be revoked, and their communication endpoints must be disabled to prevent ghost devices from being used maliciously. Failure to manage device lifecycle securely results in lingering risks that are difficult to detect and resolve.

API exposure is another serious concern. In large IoT deployments, thousands or even millions of devices may connect to a central API. This makes the API a high-value target for attackers seeking to disrupt service or exfiltrate data. Denial-of-service attacks against IoT APIs can render entire networks of devices inoperable. Therefore, APIs must be protected using web application firewalls, distributed denial-of-service mitigation services, and intelligent traffic shaping. Access to the API must be segmented by role, region, or device type to limit the impact of compromised credentials or elevated permissions. Sensitive operations such as firmware updates, device configuration, or remote command execution must be locked behind multi-factor authentication and audit logging to prevent unauthorized use.

Firmware and software updates present another attack vector. Many IoT devices support over-the-air updates delivered via APIs. If these update mechanisms are not securely implemented, attackers can push malicious firmware, install backdoors, or render devices inoperable. APIs responsible for distributing updates must validate the authenticity of update packages using digital signatures and enforce strict access controls to ensure that only verified sources can initiate an update. Devices must also validate updates locally and perform rollback checks to prevent permanent compromise. The update process must be resilient to interruptions, power failures, and network inconsistencies, as any failure could result in bricked devices or inconsistent states across the network.

Scalability introduces further challenges in API security for IoT. The volume of data generated by IoT devices and the frequency of API calls can overwhelm backend systems if not properly managed. APIs must be designed with scalability in mind, using efficient message formats, asynchronous communication, and load-balanced architectures. Caching, queuing, and batching strategies can help reduce the pressure on core systems. Security features must also scale, ensuring that every device connection is authenticated and encrypted without introducing latency or degrading performance. Monitoring and alerting systems must be capable of processing massive volumes of API telemetry to detect attacks in real time.

Another overlooked risk is the physical insecurity of IoT devices. Unlike cloud servers, which are housed in controlled environments, IoT devices are often deployed in public, remote, or hostile locations. Attackers can access the hardware directly, extract firmware, modify storage, or connect debugging interfaces. APIs that rely on the integrity of device-side logic must assume that the client can be compromised. Therefore, sensitive business logic, access control decisions, and data transformations must be enforced on the server side, with APIs performing strict validation of all inputs and behaviors. Trust boundaries must be clearly defined, and minimal trust should be placed in the device's local environment.

Regulatory and privacy concerns are growing as IoT devices collect more personal and behavioral data. APIs must support data governance requirements such as consent management, data minimization, and the right to be forgotten. Data collected from IoT devices must be mapped, classified, and handled according to applicable regulations such as GDPR, CCPA, or HIPAA. APIs must support secure data deletion, user-controlled access, and clear audit trails to demonstrate compliance. Failure to implement privacy-respecting API designs can result in legal penalties and erosion of consumer trust.

The security of APIs in IoT systems is a multifaceted challenge that spans authentication, encryption, lifecycle management, scalability, and privacy. Unlike traditional applications, IoT environments operate under constraints that require specialized solutions and careful architectural planning. APIs are the linchpins of communication in IoT, and their protection is paramount to the security of the entire ecosystem. As IoT adoption continues to expand across industries, the ability to design and maintain secure, scalable, and resilient APIs will become a defining capability for developers, architects, and security professionals tasked with defending the next generation of connected systems.

# Real-Time APIs and WebSocket Security

The demand for real-time data exchange has led to the widespread adoption of real-time APIs, particularly those powered by WebSockets. Unlike traditional RESTful APIs that operate over stateless HTTP requests, WebSockets enable full-duplex communication channels between clients and servers, allowing data to flow bidirectionally with minimal latency. This model supports use cases such as live chat, financial market feeds, multiplayer gaming, collaborative editing, and IoT telemetry. While the real-time capabilities of WebSockets provide significant user experience advantages, they also introduce unique security concerns that must be addressed from both an architectural and implementation perspective. Securing real-time APIs that use WebSockets requires a deep understanding of persistent connections, session management, data integrity, and the shifting threat landscape that arises from maintaining long-lived channels between systems.

One of the primary differences between WebSockets and HTTP-based APIs is the nature of the connection itself. With WebSockets, a single TCP connection is established and remains open, allowing data to be sent at any time without re-establishing a new request. This persistent state challenges traditional models of stateless security and demands additional mechanisms to ensure that connections remain secure throughout their lifetime. Authentication, for instance, cannot rely solely on a one-time token used during the initial handshake. Instead, session validation must be performed continuously or in response to specific triggers, such as token expiration or changes in user context. WebSocket servers must be capable of identifying each connected client reliably and maintaining a secure session state that reflects the user's identity and authorization level.

The WebSocket handshake begins with an HTTP request, which means it can leverage existing authentication infrastructure, such as token-based schemes using OAuth 2.0 or JSON Web Tokens. However, once the handshake is completed and the protocol is upgraded to WebSocket, traditional HTTP headers are no longer available, and the connection becomes a raw data stream. To maintain security, any credentials or tokens passed during the handshake must be stored securely and bound to the session for ongoing verification. Additionally, it is essential to validate that tokens are not reused, forged, or replayed. This is particularly important in public or untrusted networks where attackers might attempt to hijack connections or intercept tokens through man-in-the-middle attacks.

To prevent unauthorized access and impersonation, mutual authentication can be implemented using client-side certificates or device fingerprints. In environments with high security requirements, mutual TLS provides a strong guarantee that both the client and the server are who they claim to be. Device-based fingerprinting, on the other hand, captures characteristics such as hardware ID, operating system version, and installed software to uniquely identify each client. These identifiers can be stored and compared during reconnection attempts to detect anomalies or potential spoofing attempts. Such checks must be implemented carefully to avoid privacy violations or inadvertent tracking of legitimate users across sessions.

Encryption is mandatory for all WebSocket connections, especially those transmitting sensitive or private data. The secure version of the protocol, wss://, uses TLS to encrypt the data stream and protect it from eavesdropping or tampering. TLS must be configured using strong cipher suites and up-to-date protocols to prevent downgrade attacks and enforce forward secrecy. Certificate validation must be enforced on the client side to prevent accepting self-signed or invalid certificates, which could be used by attackers to intercept communications. Server implementations must rotate and manage certificates securely, ensuring that expiring certificates are replaced promptly and that certificate chains are validated during connection establishment.

Because WebSocket connections are long-lived, they must be monitored for timeout and inactivity conditions. Idle connections consume server resources and can be abused in denial-of-service attacks aimed at exhausting the available connection pool. To mitigate this, servers must enforce timeouts and send periodic keep-alive messages to verify that the client is still responsive. If a connection is found to be idle or unresponsive, it must be terminated gracefully, and the client must be required to reauthenticate. Similarly, connection limits should be applied per IP address, per user, or per session to prevent abuse and maintain service availability under high load.

Another major challenge in WebSocket security is input validation and message inspection. Once a WebSocket connection is established, data flows in the form of frames rather than discrete HTTP requests. Each frame may contain structured messages in formats such as JSON, XML, or binary data, and these messages must be validated just like any other user input. Servers must enforce strict schema validation, checking that each message conforms to the expected structure, data types, and value ranges. Failure to validate messages can lead to injection vulnerabilities, logic manipulation, or denial-of-service conditions. Malicious actors may send malformed or oversized frames to exploit parsing errors or buffer overflows, so limits on message size and frame count must be enforced at the protocol level.

Because WebSocket traffic does not follow the traditional request-response model, many application firewalls and intrusion detection systems are unable to parse and analyze the payloads effectively. This lack of visibility can create blind spots in security monitoring. To address this, specialized WebSocket-aware security solutions must be deployed to inspect real-time traffic, detect anomalies, and block malicious patterns. These systems must be able to decode message formats, track session state, and apply rules for detecting threats such as command injection, data exfiltration, or privilege escalation attempts. Logging is also more complex with WebSockets, as communication may consist of thousands of small messages exchanged over a single session. Logs must capture enough context to reconstruct the session history and support forensic analysis.

Authorization must be enforced at the message level, not just at the time of connection establishment. Since a single WebSocket connection can support multiple operations or data channels, each message must be evaluated to ensure that the user has the appropriate permissions for the requested action. Access control checks must be performed based on the user's role, current session state, and the nature of the data being accessed or modified. Failing to implement fine-grained authorization can result in horizontal or vertical privilege escalation, where one user is able to perform actions intended only for others or for administrators.

Finally, real-time APIs must be designed with resilience and recovery in mind. When a WebSocket connection is disrupted due to network instability, client crash, or server failure, the system must handle reconnections gracefully. Authentication and session restoration mechanisms must be in place to ensure that reconnecting clients resume operation securely and do not bypass security checks. Rate limits on reconnection attempts prevent abuse during outages or attacks. State synchronization between client and server is also critical to ensure that no data is lost, duplicated, or processed out of order. Secure recovery procedures help maintain both availability and integrity under adverse conditions.

Real-time APIs and WebSocket communication offer powerful capabilities but demand a rigorous and nuanced approach to security. The persistent nature of connections, the complexity of message parsing, and the limitations of traditional monitoring tools make WebSocket environments uniquely vulnerable to a range of threats. Developers and security engineers must work together to implement layered defenses, enforce strict validation, monitor behavior, and respond swiftly to emerging risks. Only through proactive and resilient security design can organizations ensure that their real-time APIs remain robust, trustworthy, and secure in the face of modern attack vectors.

# GraphQL Security: Queries and Mutations

GraphQL has become a popular alternative to REST for building APIs due to its flexibility and efficiency. It allows clients to request exactly the data they need, reducing over-fetching and under-fetching issues. With a single endpoint, GraphQL enables complex data retrieval and modification operations using structured queries and mutations. However, the very flexibility that makes GraphQL powerful also introduces unique security risks that must be addressed to prevent abuse, data leaks, denial-of-service attacks, and unauthorized access. Protecting GraphQL APIs requires a deep understanding of how queries and mutations work, how attackers can exploit them, and what measures developers and security teams must implement to secure the entire GraphQL stack.

Unlike REST APIs where each endpoint corresponds to a specific resource or action, GraphQL APIs expose a single endpoint that handles all operations through queries and mutations. This means that a single poorly secured GraphQL endpoint could provide access to all of the application's data and functionality. Queries are used to read data, while mutations modify it. Both types of operations can be nested and customized extensively by the client. This ability to construct arbitrarily complex operations at runtime increases the attack surface dramatically. Attackers can craft deeply nested or overly broad queries to stress backend systems, exfiltrate data, or bypass access controls.

One of the most critical security issues with GraphQL is the risk of excessive data exposure. Since GraphQL APIs often expose the entire schema to clients, including all types, fields, and relationships, clients can discover sensitive data structures that were never meant to be public. This introspection capability, while useful for developers and tooling, also provides attackers with a roadmap of the backend. If not properly restricted, introspection can be used to identify hidden objects, administrative operations, or deprecated fields that are still accessible. To mitigate this, introspection should be disabled in production environments unless strictly necessary. Alternatively, access to introspection queries can be restricted based on authentication level or IP range.

Another major concern is the issue of unauthorized access to data or functionality. Because clients define their own queries and mutations, it becomes essential to enforce fine-grained authorization checks on every field and operation. Simply verifying that a user is authenticated is not sufficient. The API must verify whether the authenticated user is authorized to access each field in the query or to perform each mutation. Without strict authorization enforcement, users could query fields they are not entitled to, such as email addresses, payment information, or internal notes. Authorization logic must be implemented at the resolver level, since each field may involve different access rules. Centralized authorization frameworks or middleware can help maintain consistency and reduce the risk of missing critical checks.

Denial-of-service attacks are another significant threat to GraphQL APIs. Because clients can construct queries of arbitrary depth and complexity, attackers can exploit this capability to consume excessive CPU, memory, or database resources. A common tactic involves crafting deeply nested queries or queries with recursive fragments that force the backend to perform expensive join operations or load large datasets. To counter this, GraphQL servers must implement query depth limiting, which restricts the maximum depth of any given query. They must also enforce query complexity limits, which assign a computational cost to each field and reject queries that exceed a predefined threshold. These measures help prevent resource exhaustion while still allowing legitimate clients to perform meaningful operations.

Input validation is just as important in GraphQL as it is in REST. Fields in mutations often accept user-provided input that modifies data in the backend. Without proper validation, these inputs can be used to exploit logic flaws, perform injection attacks, or manipulate business rules. Each input type must be validated for type, format, length, and allowed values. GraphQL's strong typing system provides some protection, but it is not a substitute for validation logic. For example, a field defined as a string will accept any string, including payloads that may be used in cross-site scripting or injection attempts. Validation should occur both at the GraphQL schema level and within application logic to ensure comprehensive coverage.

Logging and monitoring are essential components of GraphQL security. Since a single endpoint handles all operations, distinguishing between legitimate and malicious activity requires detailed logging of queries, variables, user context, and response times. Logs must be structured and stored securely, enabling security teams to analyze trends, detect anomalies, and investigate incidents. Rate limiting and throttling mechanisms must be applied to prevent abuse from automated tools or malicious users. These limits can be based on query complexity, number of requests per minute, or a combination of factors. Suspicious patterns such as repeated failed mutations, excessive query depth, or attempts to access restricted fields should trigger alerts or temporary blocks.

Error handling in GraphQL must be implemented carefully to avoid information leakage. The default behavior of many GraphQL libraries is to return detailed error messages, including stack traces, internal exception messages, and resolver failures. While useful during development, these messages can reveal implementation details that attackers might use to craft targeted attacks. In production, error messages should be sanitized and standardized to prevent leakage of internal logic. Developers must also ensure that exceptions do not inadvertently bypass security checks or cause partial data exposure.

Authentication in GraphQL is typically handled through HTTP headers, such as bearer tokens or API keys. However, it is essential to bind the authentication context to the execution of the query or mutation. This means that resolvers must have access to the authenticated user's identity and attributes and must enforce access control accordingly. Stateless authentication mechanisms such as JWTs must be validated rigorously, including signature verification, expiration checks, and scope validation. Sessions must be monitored for unusual behavior, and authentication tokens must be rotated periodically to reduce the risk of misuse.

Securing GraphQL APIs also involves schema design best practices. Developers should avoid exposing unnecessary fields or mutations, even if access is restricted. Schema pruning, which removes unused or deprecated parts of the schema, reduces the attack surface and simplifies security enforcement. Naming conventions and field organization can also help developers identify sensitive areas and apply appropriate controls. Versioning strategies, while not natively supported by GraphQL, can be implemented by maintaining separate schema branches or using custom directives to indicate field lifecycle stages.

In environments where GraphQL APIs are exposed to third parties or integrated into public-facing applications, additional precautions must be taken. Schema stitching, federation, and gateway layers can introduce additional complexity and potential vulnerabilities. Each component in the GraphQL architecture must enforce its own security policies, validate inputs, and log activity. Security testing tools must be adapted to understand the nuances of GraphQL, including the ability to generate complex queries and mutations, test resolver behavior, and detect misconfigurations.

GraphQL introduces a dynamic and powerful way to interact with APIs, but its flexibility demands a rigorous and proactive security posture. Every query and mutation represents an opportunity for misuse if not properly controlled. By implementing field-level authorization, limiting query complexity, enforcing validation, and monitoring activity continuously, developers can ensure that GraphQL APIs provide both functionality and security. As the adoption of GraphQL grows, organizations must invest in the tools, training, and practices necessary to protect their data and infrastructure from the unique risks posed by this technology.

# REST vs gRPC: Security Comparisons

As API technologies continue to evolve, two of the most widely adopted paradigms—REST and gRPC—have become central to how modern applications communicate. REST has long been the de facto standard for web APIs, offering simplicity, wide compatibility, and human readability. In contrast, gRPC is a more recent framework built on top of HTTP/2 and protocol buffers, offering high performance, streaming capabilities, and strict contract enforcement. While both approaches serve similar purposes in connecting distributed systems, their security models differ in fundamental ways. Understanding the security implications of REST and gRPC is essential for architects and developers tasked with building resilient and secure communication layers. Comparing these two paradigms from a security perspective reveals the strengths and weaknesses inherent to each and highlights the trade-offs involved in selecting one over the other.

One of the most immediate differences between REST and gRPC lies in the transport protocol and message format. REST is typically implemented over HTTP/1.1, using JSON as the message format. JSON, being human-readable and text-based, makes inspection and debugging straightforward, but it also introduces certain vulnerabilities. JSON parsers are subject to a variety of issues such as injection attacks, schema validation flaws, and parsing ambiguities. In contrast, gRPC uses HTTP/2 and encodes messages using protocol buffers, a compact binary format that is faster and less prone to structural manipulation. While this binary nature enhances performance and reduces attack surfaces like injection through malformed inputs, it also reduces transparency, making it harder to inspect and analyze traffic without specialized tooling.

Authentication mechanisms for REST APIs typically involve bearer tokens, often implemented using OAuth 2.0 and JWTs. These tokens are included in HTTP headers and can be intercepted or reused if not properly secured. Since REST is stateless, each request must be independently authenticated, which is a strength in terms of compartmentalization but can lead to inefficiencies in high-throughput environments. gRPC also supports bearer token-based authentication, but it offers a more robust model by natively supporting mutual TLS. With mTLS, both client and server authenticate each other using digital certificates during the TLS handshake, creating a higher degree of trust and a more secure channel. While mutual TLS can also be used with REST, it is not as seamlessly integrated and often requires additional configuration.

Transport encryption is mandatory for both REST and gRPC when transmitting sensitive data. REST uses HTTPS, which is HTTP over TLS, and gRPC uses HTTP/2 over TLS as a baseline. However, gRPC's reliance on HTTP/2 offers advantages in connection handling and encryption performance. HTTP/2 multiplexes multiple streams over a single connection, reducing the number of TLS handshakes and improving efficiency, especially for systems that maintain frequent bidirectional communication. This reduces exposure to TLS negotiation attacks and minimizes the chances of session hijacking through connection reuse. REST over HTTP/1.1, with its connection-per-request model, is more susceptible to certain man-in-the-middle threats if not managed properly.

In terms of authorization, REST APIs often rely on path-based access control, where different HTTP endpoints correspond to different resources and permissions are enforced at the route level. This model is straightforward but becomes complex as the number of endpoints grows. Misconfigured access controls can lead to privilege escalation or unauthorized data exposure. gRPC, with its strongly typed service definitions and method-based routing, lends itself to a more structured and centralized access control model. Each method in a gRPC service can have its own authorization logic, and access can be tied directly to the method name and request structure. This granularity, combined with protocol buffer contracts, makes it easier to enforce consistent security policies and validate inputs.

Another area of comparison is input validation and schema enforcement. In REST, data validation is typically implemented using custom middleware or external libraries, and the loose nature of JSON schemas can result in inconsistent enforcement across services. gRPC benefits from strict schema definitions enforced by protocol buffers, which require explicit field types, constraints, and serialization rules. This helps prevent common vulnerabilities such as type confusion, unexpected nulls, or parameter overflows. Moreover, protocol buffers reject fields that are not part of the defined schema, unlike JSON parsers that may silently accept and ignore unknown properties, potentially leading to undefined behavior or security gaps.

Logging and monitoring capabilities differ between the two paradigms. REST, being plain text and widely supported, integrates easily with existing log aggregation and monitoring tools. This makes it easier to track request metadata, debug issues, and identify suspicious activity. On the other hand, gRPC's binary format complicates observability. Logging raw gRPC messages requires decoding tools and structured logging formats. However, gRPC supports built-in tracing and interceptors, which can be used to collect telemetry and enforce audit logging at the method level. When properly configured, gRPC can provide highly granular logs that include message size, method execution time, and authentication context, although the complexity of setting this up is higher.

Rate limiting and abuse protection are essential for both REST and gRPC. In REST, rate limiting is commonly implemented at the API gateway or reverse proxy level, based on IP address, API key, or user identifier. Since requests are stateless and URL-based, it is easy to associate requests with specific routes and apply limits accordingly. gRPC, with its persistent connections and streaming capabilities, introduces new dimensions to rate limiting. Limits must account for connection lifetime, message frequency, and stream bandwidth, making the implementation more complex. Without proper controls, a client could open a stream and flood the server with messages or maintain idle connections that exhaust resources. Solutions such as server-side interceptors and token bucket algorithms are used to enforce fair usage and prevent denial-of-service conditions.

Error handling and message security also reveal key differences. In REST, errors are returned using standardized HTTP status codes, with optional message bodies. This provides a consistent framework for clients to interpret failures and react accordingly. gRPC, however, uses a separate set of status codes and embeds error messages in the response metadata. While this allows for richer error reporting, it also requires clients to be tightly coupled with the gRPC framework to parse and respond to failures correctly. From a security perspective, care must be taken to avoid leaking internal implementation details in error messages, especially in gRPC where binary formats may obscure what information is exposed to clients.

Ultimately, the choice between REST and gRPC from a security standpoint depends on the application context, operational requirements, and ecosystem maturity. REST offers simplicity, compatibility, and a mature tooling landscape that makes it easier to audit and enforce baseline security. gRPC, while requiring more initial setup and specialized tools, provides better performance, stronger schema enforcement, and native support for modern security features like mutual TLS and structured authorization. Developers must weigh these factors carefully and apply the appropriate security controls based on the architecture and threat model of their specific use case. In many cases, hybrid systems that use REST for public interfaces and gRPC for internal communication achieve the best of both worlds, balancing accessibility with advanced security capabilities.

# Securing Legacy APIs

Legacy APIs present one of the most complex and persistent challenges in the realm of application security. These APIs were often developed before modern security standards were established and can be tightly coupled with older systems that were not designed with current threat landscapes in mind. Despite their age, legacy APIs continue to power critical business functions and support essential client applications, making their continued availability and reliability a necessity.

However, their outdated design, lack of documentation, and inability to accommodate modern security practices leave them vulnerable to a range of threats, including injection attacks, authentication bypass, data leakage, and unauthorized access. Securing legacy APIs requires a multi-layered and pragmatic approach that respects operational constraints while incrementally introducing modern protections to reduce risk without disrupting functionality.

The first challenge in securing legacy APIs is visibility. Many legacy systems lack adequate logging, documentation, or monitoring, which makes it difficult for security teams to assess what data is exposed, who is accessing it, and how frequently it is being used. The absence of standardized metadata or access logs often means that teams must reverse-engineer functionality or rely on tribal knowledge within the organization to understand how the API operates. This discovery phase is critical because without full knowledge of the API's endpoints, parameters, and behaviors, it is impossible to apply consistent access control or to identify attack vectors. Traffic analysis tools, passive network monitoring, and application-layer proxies can be deployed to inspect and log incoming requests and outgoing responses, helping to build a comprehensive map of the API's use cases and risk surface.

Once visibility is established, the next focus must be on access control. Many legacy APIs were built in an era when authentication was an afterthought or entirely absent. Even those that implement rudimentary credential checks may use outdated methods like basic authentication over unencrypted channels or custom tokens without expiry. Where possible, legacy APIs should be placed behind an API gateway that supports modern authentication protocols such as OAuth 2.0 or API key management. The gateway acts as a choke point, enforcing authentication and authorization policies before requests reach the legacy system. This strategy allows the legacy API to remain unchanged while introducing a modern and auditable layer of access control. If the legacy system cannot be modified, the gateway may need to translate modern tokens into legacy-compatible headers or credentials, enabling seamless operation with improved security.

Transport security is another critical area. Legacy APIs often operate over plaintext HTTP or rely on outdated versions of TLS with weak cipher suites. These insecure channels can expose sensitive data to interception, manipulation, or injection by attackers with network access. Even when an API is hosted behind a corporate firewall or used only internally, the lack of encryption leaves it vulnerable to insider threats and lateral movement during breaches. All legacy APIs should be wrapped with TLS encryption using a reverse proxy or load balancer that terminates HTTPS traffic. Certificates must be issued by a trusted certificate authority and rotated regularly, and weak TLS versions must be disabled to ensure strong encryption. Even if the backend system remains unencrypted, encrypting the external traffic path significantly reduces the risk of data exposure.

Another frequent problem with legacy APIs is input validation. Many of these systems were developed without formal validation routines, trusting that client applications would submit well-formed requests. In today's security environment, this assumption is dangerous. Attackers can craft malformed requests, inject malicious payloads, or exploit type mismatches to trigger errors or manipulate system behavior. Since modifying the legacy code may not be feasible, input validation should be performed upstream, either at the API gateway or through a web application firewall that can inspect and sanitize requests. Rules should be created to enforce expected parameter types, lengths, and formats, and any deviation should result in the request being blocked or logged for analysis. Schema validation and regular expression filters can help enforce acceptable input patterns, reducing the risk of injection or buffer overflow attacks.

Rate limiting and abuse prevention are often missing from legacy APIs. Without restrictions on how frequently or in what volume clients can make requests, legacy systems can be overwhelmed by legitimate usage spikes or targeted by automated attacks. Implementing rate limiting at the gateway level protects the underlying API from resource exhaustion and supports fair usage policies. Limits can be based on client identity, IP address, or token, and should be tuned based on observed traffic patterns. Combined with logging and alerting, rate limits help detect and mitigate brute force attacks, credential stuffing, or attempts to enumerate endpoints.

Logging and monitoring must also be enhanced. Legacy APIs typically lack structured logging, and errors may not be captured consistently. By routing traffic through a modern gateway or proxy, security teams can generate standardized logs that include request paths, headers, client identities, response codes, and latency metrics. These logs can be integrated with centralized logging platforms and SIEM systems to support threat detection and incident response. In addition, anomaly detection tools can flag unusual access patterns, such as requests from unexpected geographies, sudden traffic spikes, or deviations from normal client behavior. These indicators can prompt further investigation or trigger automated defensive measures.

Where feasible, legacy APIs should be isolated from the broader network using segmentation and firewall rules. Placing legacy systems in their own subnet or VLAN, accessible only through specific entry points, limits the exposure in case of compromise. The principle of least privilege should guide access control decisions, ensuring that only authorized clients and services can reach the API. Outbound traffic from the legacy system should also be restricted to prevent data exfiltration or communication with command-and-control servers in the event of a breach. Microsegmentation and host-based firewalls offer additional control, especially in hybrid or cloud environments where legacy systems may coexist with modern applications.

Finally, a long-term strategy must be developed for either modernizing or decommissioning the legacy API. Security patches, even if infrequent, should be applied wherever possible, and any known vulnerabilities must be mitigated through external controls or compensating mechanisms. Legacy APIs that cannot be updated must be carefully monitored and gradually replaced with modern equivalents that support strong authentication, encryption, and structured access control. This transition should be planned with clear milestones, including migration of clients, verification of data parity, and performance benchmarking. Until that transition is complete, legacy APIs must be treated as high-risk components requiring heightened attention, layered defenses, and rigorous audit practices.

Securing legacy APIs is an ongoing process that demands creativity, patience, and a commitment to continuous improvement. While the constraints of aging infrastructure and limited development resources pose real obstacles, modern tools and architectural patterns make it possible to reduce risk significantly without disrupting core functionality. By wrapping, monitoring, and enforcing security controls externally, organizations can protect critical legacy APIs while working toward a more secure and modern application landscape.

# DevSecOps and API Security Integration

The evolution of application development has given rise to the DevSecOps movement, a practice that seeks to integrate security into every phase of the software development lifecycle rather than treating it as an afterthought. This philosophy is particularly relevant for API security, given the central role APIs play in enabling application functionality, data exchange, and system integration. APIs are often the first point of contact between services, applications, users, and even external partners. As a result, they are prime targets for attackers and must be protected with the same rigor as any critical system component. DevSecOps offers a framework for building, testing, and deploying secure APIs by embedding security tools, practices, and mindset into automated workflows and team responsibilities.

One of the foundational principles of DevSecOps is the concept of shifting security left. This means addressing security concerns during the earliest stages of development rather than postponing them until post-deployment audits or penetration tests. For APIs, this begins with secure design practices. Developers must evaluate how endpoints are structured, what data they expose, and how access is controlled. Threat modeling becomes a crucial exercise, helping teams identify potential vulnerabilities such as improper authentication, broken object-level authorization, injection points, and excessive data exposure. By involving security professionals during the design phase, teams can mitigate many common API vulnerabilities before a single line of code is written.

Code reviews and static analysis form the next layer of defense. In a DevSecOps pipeline, automated static application security testing tools are integrated directly into version control and build systems. These tools scan API code for insecure patterns, deprecated functions, and common vulnerabilities like insecure deserialization or improper input validation. In the context of APIs, special attention must be paid to how data is parsed, how authentication tokens are handled, and how user input is processed. Developers receive immediate feedback on potential security issues, allowing them to fix problems early while the cost and complexity of remediation are still low. This also promotes a culture of security awareness among developers, reducing reliance on isolated security teams.

Beyond static analysis, software composition analysis plays a critical role in securing APIs. APIs frequently depend on third-party libraries and open-source frameworks, which may introduce vulnerabilities if not properly managed. DevSecOps pipelines incorporate tools that automatically scan dependencies, cross-reference them with known vulnerability databases, and flag outdated or insecure packages. This is especially important for APIs, where a vulnerability in an authentication library or serialization component can have cascading effects across all consuming services. These tools can also enforce policies to block builds that contain high-severity vulnerabilities, ensuring that no insecure code progresses through the pipeline unnoticed.

Dynamic analysis complements static scanning by evaluating API behavior during runtime. In a DevSecOps model, APIs are deployed to staging environments where automated tests simulate real-world usage. Dynamic application security testing tools interact with the API, sending crafted requests to identify flaws such as broken access controls, insecure redirects, or information leakage. These tools analyze how the API responds to unexpected inputs, missing tokens, or malformed requests, providing valuable insights into vulnerabilities that cannot be detected through static code inspection alone. Integration with continuous integration and deployment pipelines ensures that dynamic testing occurs with every release, maintaining a consistent level of scrutiny.

Security does not end with deployment. In DevSecOps, the production environment is continuously monitored to detect anomalies, enforce policies, and respond to incidents in real time. For APIs, this means logging all access attempts, tracking authentication events, measuring latency and error rates, and detecting suspicious patterns such as unusual geographic access or rapid bursts of traffic. These metrics are collected by observability tools and forwarded to security information and event management platforms, where they are analyzed for signs of compromise. Alerts can be generated automatically, triggering incident response workflows that isolate the affected systems, revoke compromised tokens, or initiate further investigation.

Secrets management is another critical area where DevSecOps principles enhance API security. APIs often require credentials to access databases, cloud services, or third-party systems. Hardcoding these credentials in code or configuration files is a significant risk. DevSecOps pipelines integrate secret management tools that store sensitive information in encrypted vaults and inject them securely into the runtime environment. These tools support automatic rotation, granular access control, and auditing, ensuring that credentials are never exposed unnecessarily. APIs retrieve secrets at runtime using short-lived tokens or environment-specific scopes, reducing the risk of credential leakage.

Automated policy enforcement is a hallmark of mature DevSecOps implementations. Infrastructure as code templates define not just application configurations but also security controls. Policies can specify that all API endpoints must be protected by TLS, that authentication is required for all requests, or that certain endpoints are restricted to internal traffic only. These policies are validated automatically during pipeline execution, and violations result in build failures or deployment blocks. By treating security policies as code, organizations ensure that every environment is consistently secured and that any drift from baseline configurations is detected and corrected.

Continuous education and collaboration between development, operations, and security teams are essential to sustaining a DevSecOps approach to API security. Security champions can be embedded within development teams to bridge the gap between engineering goals and compliance requirements. Regular training sessions, workshops, and knowledge-sharing initiatives keep teams informed about emerging threats, best practices, and new tools. Post-incident reviews and retrospectives help teams learn from security events, refine their processes, and adapt their controls to evolving risks.

DevSecOps also supports a test-driven approach to security. Unit tests, integration tests, and end-to-end tests can be extended to include security assertions. For example, tests can verify that sensitive endpoints reject unauthenticated requests, that rate limiting is enforced, or that error messages do not reveal implementation details. These tests are executed automatically during every build, providing ongoing assurance that security requirements are being met. As the API evolves, the test suite evolves with it, maintaining a living contract that defines and enforces security expectations.

Integrating API security into a DevSecOps pipeline transforms security from a bottleneck into a continuous and proactive function. Security becomes a shared responsibility, embedded in the tools, culture, and workflows that drive application delivery. APIs benefit from this integration by becoming more resilient, more auditable, and more aligned with organizational risk management goals. Rather than being bolted on at the end, security is woven into every commit, build, test, and deployment, enabling teams to move quickly without sacrificing protection. In an era where APIs are central to digital transformation, adopting DevSecOps is no longer optional—it is essential for building secure, scalable, and trustworthy systems.

# Secrets Management in API Workflows

In modern API workflows, secrets management plays a central role in safeguarding the confidentiality and integrity of communication between services, applications, and infrastructure. APIs frequently interact with databases, third-party services, cloud providers, and internal systems that require authentication using sensitive credentials such as API keys, passwords, tokens, certificates, and encryption keys. If these secrets are mishandled, hardcoded into source code, exposed in logs, or stored in configuration files without proper protections, they become a critical point of vulnerability. An attacker who gains access to exposed secrets can impersonate services, exfiltrate data, pivot across environments, and cause widespread compromise. Therefore, implementing robust secrets management practices is not only essential for securing API workflows but also for maintaining trust and compliance in any digital system.

A foundational principle of secrets management is that secrets must never be stored in source code repositories. Code is often shared among developers, integrated with continuous integration pipelines, or made public accidentally. Even private repositories can be cloned, audited, or compromised. Once a secret is committed to a repository, it remains in the version history indefinitely unless explicit action is taken to scrub it. Automated tools exist to scan repositories for exposed secrets, and attackers often use these tools to search public repositories for credentials that grant access to sensitive systems. Therefore, secrets must be separated from the codebase entirely and handled through secure, external mechanisms that support dynamic injection and strict access control.

In API workflows, the most secure way to handle secrets is through a centralized secrets management system. These systems, such as HashiCorp Vault, AWS Secrets Manager, Azure Key Vault, and Google Secret Manager, provide secure storage, encryption at rest, fine-grained access control, audit logging, and automatic rotation capabilities. Secrets are stored in encrypted form and retrieved at runtime using authenticated and authorized requests. This architecture decouples the lifecycle of secrets from the applications that use them, enabling security teams to manage, monitor, and revoke secrets independently of application deployments. For API services, this means that database credentials, signing keys, and third-party API tokens can be updated centrally without changing application code or configuration files.

Access control is a core component of secrets management. Each API or service must be granted the minimum level of access required to perform its function, following the principle of least privilege. Access to secrets is governed by policies that define who can read, write, or delete specific secrets and under what conditions. These policies can be based on identity attributes such as roles, groups, environment, or network location. For example, a staging environment API should not have access to production credentials, and a frontend service should not be able to retrieve backend database passwords. Secrets management platforms integrate with identity providers to authenticate services using tokens, certificates, or federated identities. This integration ensures that only verified entities can retrieve secrets and that any access is logged and traceable.

One of the most critical advantages of centralized secrets management is automatic rotation. Static secrets pose a long-term risk because they can be stolen and used until manually revoked. Rotating secrets periodically reduces the window of opportunity for misuse and helps meet compliance requirements. Secrets management systems can generate new credentials automatically, update dependent systems, and revoke old credentials without manual intervention. This rotation can occur on a fixed schedule, in response to an event such as a policy violation, or when a user or system is deprovisioned. For APIs, this means that keys and tokens can be kept fresh without requiring downtime or redeployment, preserving availability while enhancing security.

Runtime injection is another important strategy in secrets management. Instead of passing secrets through environment variables, which can be accessed by any process in the system, secrets can be injected directly into memory or mounted as temporary files with restricted permissions. Some orchestration platforms such as Kubernetes support integration with secrets management systems to inject secrets into containers at runtime. These secrets are stored in temporary volumes or exposed via internal APIs and are never persisted to disk. When a container is terminated, the secrets disappear with it. This ephemeral nature of secrets ensures that credentials are not inadvertently leaked or persisted in logs or system snapshots.

Logging and auditing are vital to maintaining visibility into secrets usage. Every request to retrieve, update, or revoke a secret should be logged with metadata including the identity of the requester, timestamp, secret name, and action taken. These logs must be protected against tampering and integrated into centralized security information and event management systems. Continuous monitoring of these logs can detect anomalous behavior, such as repeated access attempts, retrievals from unexpected locations, or access by decommissioned services. Security teams can set up alerts and automated workflows to respond to suspicious activity, enabling proactive defense against credential abuse.

API developers must also adopt secure practices when integrating with secrets. Applications should retrieve secrets just-in-time, only when needed, and should never log, cache, or display them in error messages.

Sensitive operations that involve secrets, such as signing tokens or establishing secure connections, must be implemented using well-tested libraries that handle key storage and memory management securely. Developers must avoid reinventing cryptographic protocols or handling raw secret data unless absolutely necessary. When secrets must be transmitted between systems, they should be encrypted in transit using TLS and protected by authentication to prevent man-in-the-middle attacks.

Testing and development workflows require special consideration. Developers often need access to test credentials or mock secrets to build and debug applications. However, these test secrets must be strictly isolated from production environments and must never be promoted to production use. Secrets management platforms support the creation of dynamic or ephemeral secrets for testing purposes, which can be destroyed automatically after use. Sandboxed environments can simulate API behavior with fake data and controlled secrets, enabling development without risking exposure of real credentials.

As organizations scale and adopt microservices, cloud-native architectures, and continuous delivery, the need for automated and secure secrets management becomes even more pressing. API workflows span multiple environments, cloud providers, and runtime platforms, each with its own security constraints. A centralized and standardized approach to secrets ensures consistency, reduces the risk of human error, and enables rapid response to incidents. Secrets management is no longer a task limited to operations or security teams—it must be integrated into the development lifecycle, supported by tooling, and embraced as a shared responsibility.

Managing secrets securely is fundamental to the integrity and reliability of API ecosystems. By treating secrets as dynamic, protected resources rather than static configuration values, organizations can build systems that are resilient to compromise, compliant with regulatory standards, and capable of supporting secure innovation at scale. As the complexity of application environments increases, so too must the maturity of the secrets management practices that underpin them. APIs that integrate robust secrets management not only protect sensitive information but also lay the foundation for secure and trustworthy digital experiences.


# Supply Chain Risks in API Dependencies

Modern API development relies heavily on open-source libraries, third-party SDKs, public packages, and commercial integrations to accelerate development and reduce the burden of building complex features from scratch. This ecosystem of dependencies forms what is known as the software supply chain. While this model offers immense productivity benefits, it also introduces significant security risks that organizations must confront. The trust placed in upstream dependencies can be exploited by attackers, who target popular packages or inject malicious code into lesser-known modules to compromise entire applications. In the context of API development, supply chain risks can manifest in vulnerabilities that enable remote code execution, data leakage, authentication bypass, and the unauthorized manipulation of critical business logic. APIs, being the interface to sensitive services and data, are especially vulnerable when their dependencies are not rigorously vetted and monitored.

One of the most dangerous aspects of supply chain risk is transitive dependencies. Developers may directly include only a handful of libraries, but each of those libraries may, in turn, import dozens or even hundreds of other modules. These transitive dependencies often escape scrutiny because they are not explicitly declared by the application itself, yet they have the same level of access and execution as top-level dependencies. A vulnerability in one of these downstream components can go undetected for months, quietly exposing the API to attackers. In some cases, attackers deliberately compromise low-profile packages that are included in widely used frameworks, using them as a delivery mechanism for malicious payloads. These payloads can be designed to activate under specific conditions, making detection even more difficult.

Malicious packages represent another major threat in the API supply chain. Attackers may publish software libraries with names that closely resemble legitimate packages, hoping that developers will install them by mistake. This technique, known as typosquatting, has been successfully used to infiltrate codebases with malicious components that exfiltrate environment variables, open reverse shells, or modify API responses. Even official package repositories like npm, PyPI, or Maven Central are not immune to such threats. When these malicious packages are integrated into an API, they can compromise authentication tokens, extract sensitive request data, or alter logic used in critical operations. Since APIs often deal with user identity, financial transactions, and confidential data exchange, the consequences of such compromise are severe.

Even well-maintained libraries can become liabilities if they are no longer actively supported. Abandoned dependencies receive no security updates, leaving them vulnerable to newly discovered exploits. In some cases, attackers have taken over abandoned packages by assuming ownership of dormant accounts or submitting patches that introduce backdoors. These updates may appear benign at first glance, passing automated tests and review processes, only to activate under targeted conditions. This highlights the importance of tracking not only the version of each dependency but also the history, maintainers, and update frequency. APIs that rely on stagnant or poorly maintained libraries risk inheriting vulnerabilities that are silently exploited.

Dependency confusion is another technique that has emerged as a potent attack vector. In this scenario, internal applications use private package registries with specific naming conventions. Attackers publish public packages with the same names to public registries, hoping that the build or deployment system will pull the public version instead of the intended private one. If the public package contains malicious code, the application unknowingly integrates it and deploys a compromised version. For APIs, this can lead to the exposure of internal endpoints, the elevation of privileges, or the redirection of data to attacker-controlled systems. To prevent dependency confusion, developers must configure their package managers to resolve dependencies from authenticated sources and verify the integrity of every downloaded component.

Mitigating supply chain risk in API development requires a combination of technical controls, process improvements, and cultural awareness. At the technical level, organizations must implement software composition analysis tools that scan all dependencies, including transitive ones, for known vulnerabilities. These tools compare package versions against vulnerability databases and alert developers when insecure components are in use. Integration with CI/CD pipelines ensures that no new code is merged or deployed without first passing dependency checks. Additionally, tools that generate software bills of materials help teams understand exactly which components are in use and support rapid response when new vulnerabilities are disclosed.

Dependency pinning is another critical practice. By locking dependencies to specific, known-safe versions, developers can prevent unexpected updates from introducing breaking changes or new vulnerabilities. However, pinning must be accompanied by scheduled review and update processes, as relying indefinitely on old versions can leave APIs exposed to known threats. Automated dependency management tools can help by opening pull requests when new versions are available, enabling teams to test and review changes in a controlled manner.

Code signing and checksum verification add another layer of defense. When downloading packages, verifying digital signatures or cryptographic hashes ensures that the component has not been tampered with. Although not all package managers support this out of the box, organizations can enforce verification steps as part of their build process. For APIs, this is especially relevant when integrating critical components such as authentication libraries, encryption modules, or payment processors. Trusting these components without validation exposes APIs to systemic failure.

Vendor risk must also be considered when APIs rely on commercial or SaaS-provided SDKs. Even trusted vendors can introduce risks through poorly maintained SDKs, insecure API gateways, or inadequate data protection practices. Evaluating the security posture of vendors, understanding how their libraries integrate with the application, and monitoring updates from these providers is essential. APIs that serve regulated industries must ensure that any third-party integration complies with relevant standards and undergoes regular security assessments.

Security education is a powerful tool in reducing supply chain risks. Developers must be trained to recognize risky practices, such as downloading libraries from unverified sources, disabling dependency warnings, or failing to verify package authenticity. They must also understand how to read vulnerability reports and what actions to take when a component in their API stack is found to be vulnerable. Cultivating a mindset of zero trust toward external dependencies, even those that are widely used and highly rated, helps prevent blind faith in components that may contain hidden threats.

The API supply chain is vast, dynamic, and inherently complex. It reflects the interconnected nature of modern software development, where no application is truly built in isolation. Every dependency is a potential entry point for attackers and a shared responsibility for the teams that build and maintain APIs. As threats become more sophisticated and as APIs continue to power critical services, the need to manage supply chain risk becomes not only a security imperative but a foundational requirement for resilient and trustworthy digital systems.

# Managing Third-Party API Integrations Securely

Third-party API integrations have become indispensable in modern application development. Whether it is integrating with payment gateways, identity providers, communication platforms, analytics tools, or cloud services, organizations rely heavily on external APIs to extend functionality, accelerate development, and improve user experiences. While these integrations offer significant advantages, they also introduce a wide range of security risks. Each third-party API represents a potential point of vulnerability that, if not properly secured, can become a conduit for data breaches, service disruptions, and unauthorized access. Managing third-party API integrations securely is therefore a critical aspect of an organization's overall security posture, demanding careful planning, strict control, and continuous monitoring.

The first step toward secure integration is performing due diligence before selecting a third-party API provider. This involves assessing the provider's reputation, security practices, compliance certifications, data handling policies, and history of vulnerabilities or breaches. Not all APIs are created equal, and a decision to integrate with a poorly secured API can have long-term repercussions. Security-conscious organizations must treat third-party providers as extensions of their own infrastructure and subject them to the same level of scrutiny they would apply to internal systems. This assessment includes understanding how the provider authenticates clients, how it transmits data, whether it encrypts data at rest and in transit, how it handles errors, and what controls are in place for rate limiting and abuse prevention.

Authentication and authorization are foundational to securing third-party API usage. Integrations must always use strong, verifiable authentication mechanisms such as OAuth 2.0 or API keys issued with scopes and expiration policies. Static keys with unrestricted access are particularly dangerous, as they can be leaked, reused, or exploited without triggering alarms. Whenever possible, integrations should use short-lived tokens tied to specific scopes that define exactly what actions the calling application can perform. These scopes should be limited to the minimum set of permissions necessary for the integration to function. Excessive permissions expand the potential blast radius if the token is compromised. Additionally, tokens and credentials should never be stored in code repositories or hardcoded into applications. Secure secret management systems must be used to store and inject them at runtime, and access to these secrets should be restricted and logged.

Secure communication is essential when interacting with third-party APIs. All data exchanges must be conducted over HTTPS with TLS to ensure encryption in transit. Applications must validate the provider's TLS certificate and reject connections that fail validation or that use deprecated or insecure protocols. Certificate pinning can add an extra layer of protection, ensuring that communication occurs only with trusted endpoints. While TLS protects the channel, it does not guarantee the integrity of the response. Therefore, applications should implement mechanisms to validate and sanitize all data received from third-party APIs, especially if that data is passed on to users or other systems. Blindly trusting external data can lead to injection vulnerabilities, logic errors, or data corruption.

Rate limiting and error handling are other areas that require careful design. Third-party APIs may enforce usage quotas, throttle high-volume requests, or return different types of error messages based on request content. Applications must be resilient to these behaviors and avoid tight coupling with external APIs that could cause cascading failures. Implementing retry logic with exponential backoff, circuit breakers, and fallback mechanisms ensures that temporary outages or delays in third-party APIs do not disrupt the core functionality of the application. Moreover, logs must capture error responses and unusual patterns of API usage so that potential issues can be diagnosed and addressed quickly.

Third-party APIs must be integrated in a way that preserves user privacy and complies with data protection regulations. Before sending any user data to an external API, applications must confirm that such data transfers are permitted and that users have given appropriate consent. Sensitive data such as personally identifiable information, payment details, or health records must be encrypted, minimized, and handled in accordance with applicable laws such as GDPR, CCPA, or HIPAA. Organizations should consider data anonymization or pseudonymization techniques where possible and must ensure that data sent to third-party APIs is adequately protected both during transmission and while at rest in the third party's environment.

Visibility and monitoring are critical for maintaining control over third-party API integrations. All requests to and responses from external APIs should be logged with sufficient detail to support auditing and incident response. This includes timestamps, endpoints called, response times, error codes, and associated user sessions or identifiers. These logs must be stored securely, protected against tampering, and monitored for anomalies. For example, a sudden spike in requests to a specific endpoint, repeated authentication failures, or an unusual pattern of data access could indicate abuse or compromise. Integrating logs with a centralized monitoring or SIEM system allows for real-time alerts and forensic analysis when suspicious activity is detected.

Access control is another pillar of secure integration. Applications that interface with third-party APIs must isolate those integrations using principles such as network segmentation, process isolation, and least privilege. For instance, if an application module is responsible for sending notifications via a third-party messaging API, it should not also have access to user data or internal system controls that are unrelated to its function. Role-based or service-level access policies must be applied at every layer, ensuring that even if a third-party token or API is compromised, the damage is contained.

Change management and version control of third-party APIs must not be overlooked. Providers may introduce breaking changes, deprecate endpoints, or alter the format of responses with little warning. To manage this, applications must track the version of the API they are using and be notified of upcoming changes through official release notes, mailing lists, or service dashboards. API gateways, proxies, or abstraction layers can help isolate the application from sudden changes, translating or adapting requests and responses to match expected formats. By maintaining compatibility through controlled interfaces, organizations reduce the risk of sudden outages or functional regressions caused by upstream changes.

Vendor lock-in and operational dependencies must also be considered. If a third-party API becomes unavailable, is acquired, or changes its business model, the impact on the consuming application can be severe. To mitigate this risk, applications should minimize coupling and design integrations that can be replaced or swapped with alternative providers. Abstracting the API functionality into internal interfaces, using open standards, and documenting integration logic make transitions more manageable. Backup providers or contingency plans should be developed for critical third-party services, particularly those involved in authentication, payments, or communications.

Managing third-party API integrations securely is a continuous process that extends beyond initial implementation. It involves risk assessment, architectural design, policy enforcement, real-time monitoring, and proactive response. The convenience and power of third-party APIs must be balanced with a thorough understanding of the associated security challenges. By implementing strong controls, adhering to best practices, and maintaining vigilant oversight, organizations can leverage the benefits of external APIs without compromising the integrity or security of their systems. APIs are not just points of integration—they are gateways into the application's ecosystem and must be treated with the highest level of caution and respect.

# Continuous API Security Assessment

As the digital landscape evolves rapidly, APIs have emerged as the core of modern software architecture, powering web applications, mobile apps, microservices, and third-party integrations. The reliance on APIs has significantly increased the attack surface for organizations, making them a prime target for cyber threats. Traditional security assessments, performed only during the development phase or at fixed intervals, are no longer sufficient to address the dynamic and constantly shifting nature of API deployments. Continuous API security assessment is a proactive and ongoing process that integrates security validation into every stage of the API lifecycle. It ensures that vulnerabilities are identified, addressed, and monitored continuously, thereby reducing the window of exposure and enabling faster incident response.

The first element of a continuous API security assessment strategy is visibility. It is impossible to protect what cannot be seen. Organizations must maintain an accurate and up-to-date inventory of all APIs in use, both internal and external. Shadow APIs, which are undocumented or unknown to the security team, pose a significant risk because they often bypass standard security controls. Discovery tools that monitor network traffic, scan repositories, and analyze runtime environments can help detect these hidden APIs and bring them under governance. Every API, once discovered, should be cataloged with metadata including its endpoints, authentication requirements, version history, and associated business functions. This inventory becomes the foundation upon which security assessments are planned and prioritized.

Once APIs are cataloged, automated tools can be deployed to perform static and dynamic analysis continuously. Static analysis tools inspect the source code, configuration files, and API definitions such as

OpenAPI or GraphQL schemas to identify insecure patterns, deprecated methods, missing validations, and hardcoded secrets. These tools are typically integrated into the CI/CD pipeline, providing feedback to developers at the time of code commit or pull request. By embedding static checks early in the development process, teams can catch and fix issues before they reach production, reducing both cost and risk.

Dynamic analysis complements static analysis by evaluating the API during execution. It simulates real-world interactions with the API, sending crafted requests to test for vulnerabilities such as injection attacks, broken access controls, insecure direct object references, and data exposure. Unlike static analysis, dynamic testing reveals how the API actually behaves under specific conditions. Continuous dynamic testing is achieved by integrating security scanners into the staging and production environments. These scanners run periodically or are triggered by specific events such as a new deployment, a configuration change, or the detection of a new endpoint. The results of these tests feed into dashboards and alerting systems, enabling teams to prioritize remediation efforts based on severity and impact.

Continuous API security assessment also involves monitoring authentication and authorization mechanisms. These controls are often the last line of defense between an attacker and sensitive data. Misconfigurations, overly permissive access, and token reuse are common issues that compromise API security. Identity-aware monitoring tools track how tokens are issued, used, and expired. They detect anomalies such as token misuse, login attempts from unexpected locations, or excessive access to specific endpoints. Continuous assessment includes regular audits of access policies to ensure that they align with the principle of least privilege. Roles, scopes, and claims must be evaluated to confirm that users and services have only the permissions they need and nothing more.

Change detection is another critical component. APIs evolve over time as new features are added, endpoints are deprecated, and integrations are updated. Each change introduces the potential for new vulnerabilities or regressions in security posture. Continuous assessment includes automated tools that monitor API definitions and compare them against previous versions to identify changes in behavior, data exposure, or required permissions. A newly added endpoint may inadvertently expose sensitive data or bypass existing security filters. Detecting such changes in real-time allows organizations to perform targeted assessments and prevent security gaps from reaching production unnoticed.

Logging and observability play a crucial role in the continuous assessment model. Every API request and response should be logged with metadata including the method, parameters, user identity, response code, and latency. These logs must be collected, normalized, and analyzed by security information and event management systems to detect suspicious behavior. Anomalies such as spikes in traffic, repeated failed logins, or unusual data access patterns may indicate reconnaissance activity or an ongoing attack. Continuous analysis of log data enables early threat detection and supports rapid response. Logs also provide the forensic evidence needed to investigate incidents and verify compliance with regulatory requirements.

Penetration testing, while traditionally performed manually and periodically, can also be adapted into the continuous model. By using automated frameworks and attack simulations, organizations can continuously challenge their APIs with a wide range of attack vectors. These tools emulate real-world threats, from credential stuffing to parameter tampering, and provide insights into how well the API can resist exploitation. When combined with threat intelligence feeds, these assessments can be updated to reflect the latest tactics used by adversaries, ensuring that defenses are tested against current threats and not just outdated vulnerabilities.

Continuous security assessment also extends to third-party and partner APIs. Organizations must monitor the behavior and reliability of the APIs they consume, especially those that handle sensitive data or critical business functions. Tools that validate the security headers, TLS configurations, and error handling behaviors of third-party APIs help ensure that integrations do not introduce downstream risks. In some cases, mutual agreements and SLAs must include provisions for security audits and assessments, allowing organizations to hold their partners accountable for maintaining a secure posture.

Education and culture are essential enablers of continuous assessment. Developers, operations teams, and security engineers must understand the importance of API security and be equipped with the tools and training necessary to contribute to the process. Security champions embedded within development teams can act as liaisons, promoting secure coding practices and assisting with the interpretation of assessment results. Continuous assessment thrives in environments where security is seen not as a gatekeeper but as a shared responsibility woven into the fabric of the development lifecycle.

Ultimately, continuous API security assessment transforms security from a one-time checklist into a living, breathing process that adapts to change, detects threats in real time, and reinforces trust in the systems that power modern applications. By embracing automation, observability, and collaboration, organizations can secure their APIs at scale and maintain a resilient posture in the face of an ever-changing threat landscape. This continuous vigilance ensures that APIs remain not only functional and performant but also robust against the sophisticated attacks that target today's interconnected systems.

# Future Trends in API Security and Protocols

As digital transformation accelerates and the API economy becomes increasingly central to modern business operations, the future of API security and protocols is set to evolve dramatically. APIs no longer serve merely as back-end interfaces for isolated systems; they have become critical connectors between services, platforms, applications, users, and devices across public and private networks. With this growing importance comes a corresponding increase in security complexity. Attackers are more sophisticated, systems are more distributed, and compliance expectations are more demanding. In the face of this changing landscape, the future of API security will be shaped by a combination of architectural shifts, advanced automation, protocol innovation, and a more nuanced understanding of trust and identity in a hyper-connected world.

One of the most significant trends is the move toward more intelligent, context-aware API security. Traditional approaches to API protection have relied heavily on static rules, fixed authentication mechanisms, and perimeter-based access controls. However, with the increasing adoption of microservices, multi-cloud architectures, edge computing, and serverless deployments, static models are proving insufficient. Future API security will be driven by dynamic policy enforcement that adapts based on user behavior, device posture, location, and risk signals. Identity and access management systems will become deeply integrated with AI-powered engines that can evaluate access requests in real-time, weighing contextual factors to make more informed decisions. This context-aware security model will reduce false positives and negatives while enabling more flexible and granular control over who can access what, when, and how.

Another major evolution lies in the protocols themselves. While REST over HTTP remains dominant today, the limitations of stateless communication and unstructured data exchange are pushing organizations to explore more efficient and secure alternatives. Protocols like gRPC and GraphQL are already gaining traction for their performance, strong typing, and flexibility. In the future, we can expect these protocols to evolve further with built-in security primitives. gRPC may integrate more robust mutual authentication and encrypted metadata exchange mechanisms. GraphQL implementations will likely adopt standardized validation layers that enforce access control at the field level, reducing the risk of over-fetching or data leakage. New protocols purpose-built for asynchronous communication and event-driven systems will also emerge, designed with security and scalability as core features rather than afterthoughts.

Zero Trust architecture is poised to redefine the security boundaries of APIs. Instead of assuming that traffic within a network is trustworthy, Zero Trust models treat every request as potentially hostile and require continuous verification. This paradigm will become essential in API design, particularly for services that span multiple environments or integrate with external providers. Future APIs will authenticate not just users but also devices, workloads, and services, using attributes such as device health, session history, and cryptographic attestation. Policy engines will evaluate each request independently, enforcing real-time decisions that adapt to the risk profile of the interaction. This model will also necessitate changes in how API gateways and service meshes function, as they will need to enforce policies at a much more granular level and work in tandem with identity providers to verify each interaction.

API security automation will expand dramatically with the advancement of DevSecOps and the increasing maturity of AI and machine learning technologies. Continuous security scanning, threat detection, anomaly analysis, and response orchestration will be automated end to end. Machine learning models will analyze vast datasets of API usage patterns, identifying deviations that may indicate credential stuffing, business logic abuse, or bot-driven attacks. These insights will feed into automated remediation pipelines, enabling systems to revoke tokens, quarantine services, or modify access policies in near real time. Predictive analytics will play a greater role in anticipating threats before they manifest, driven by historical data, threat intelligence, and simulated attack models. These capabilities will allow organizations to move from reactive to proactive API defense strategies.

The convergence of API security with broader data governance and compliance requirements will also drive future changes. Regulations such as GDPR, CCPA, HIPAA, and emerging data privacy laws around the world are compelling organizations to embed data protection into their API designs. In the future, APIs will not only enforce access controls but also apply data classification, consent management, and retention policies dynamically. Security tools will be capable of tagging sensitive data flows, blocking unauthorized exports, and logging access for audit trails with minimal manual intervention. Compliance enforcement will be embedded directly into the API infrastructure, ensuring that privacy rules are upheld without degrading performance or reliability.

Quantum computing presents another emerging frontier with potential implications for API security. While still in its infancy, quantum advancements threaten to break traditional cryptographic algorithms that underpin secure communication. Future-proofing API protocols will require the adoption of quantum-resistant cryptography, and forward-thinking organizations are already exploring post-quantum cryptographic libraries. Over time, APIs will need to support new key exchange methods and encryption algorithms that can withstand the processing power of quantum machines. This shift will demand updates across all layers of API infrastructure, from client libraries and gateways to identity providers and key management services.

Another anticipated development is the rise of self-defending APIs. These APIs will be equipped with embedded security functions that monitor their own behavior, assess incoming requests, detect misuse, and take protective action autonomously. Built-in rate limiting, schema validation, threat scoring, and policy enforcement will become the norm, reducing reliance on external proxies or security appliances. These self-defending APIs will integrate seamlessly with centralized policy orchestration platforms, allowing administrators to define high-level security objectives while APIs handle enforcement locally and intelligently. The integration of runtime application self-protection into API frameworks will further enhance this model, providing near-instantaneous mitigation of certain classes of attacks without human intervention.

The future will also witness broader adoption of secure API design patterns and contract-driven development. Instead of implementing security as an external layer, developers will define security expectations as part of the API contract itself. Tools will automatically generate policies from OpenAPI or GraphQL specifications, ensuring that endpoint-level security is tightly coupled with application logic. These contracts will include schema validation, rate limits, data masking, and access control rules that are enforced consistently across development, testing, and production environments. Combined with formal verification methods, contract-driven development will improve confidence in API reliability and security.

As APIs continue to proliferate across every industry and every layer of the digital stack, their security will become an increasingly central concern for both technology leaders and regulators. The trends that define the future of API security and protocols reflect a broader shift toward resilience, automation, intelligence, and trust minimization. Rather than relying on perimeter defenses and periodic audits, organizations will embrace continuous protection, real-time decision-making, and integrated risk management. This transformation will not only secure APIs but will also enable innovation by creating environments where developers can build, deploy, and scale services with confidence that their APIs are secure by design and resilient by default.